CW00968554

Baptism and the Distinction of the Covenants

Thomas Patient

d. 1666

Patient, Rev. Thomas, was born in England, and educated, we have no doubt, in Oxford or Cambridge. He became a Congregationalist, and emigrated to New England. After laboring in the ministry on this side of the Atlantic, he was convinced that the Saviour and his apostles were Baptists, and he frankly avowed his convictions. He was immediately subjected to violent persecutions, and to escape them he returned to England . . . .In 1640 he was appointed co-pastor with Mr. Kiffin in London, where he labored for some time . . . . In the capital of Ireland he became a very popular preacher . . . . He was on friendly relations with Oliver Cromwell himself . . . . Mr. Patient baptized a large number of persons in Dublin. He was a wise and experienced Christian, and he rendered substantial service to the Saviour's kingdom in Ireland. He died July 30, 1666, and the Lord was with him as he passed from this world of the dying into the heaven of the living. His only published work was a quarto volume on baptism.

—William Cathcart, *The Baptist Encyclopedia* (Philadelphia: L. H. Everts, 1881), 886.

*It should be noted that Thomas Patient was a signatory of the First London Baptist Confession of Faith (1644)

BAPTISM

and the

DISTINCTION *of the* COVENANTS

THOMAS PATIENT

EDITED BY

QUINN R. MOSIER

BAPTIST HERITAGE PRESS

KANSAS CITY, MO

THE

Doctrine of Baptifm,

And the Diftinction of the

C O V E N A N T S

OR A

Plain Treatife , wherein the four Effentials of

B A P T I S M,

Viz. {
 1. *Who is a Lawfull Minifter thereof ;*
 2. *What is the true Form thereof ;*
 3. *Into whofe name it is to be adminiftred ;*
 4. *Who is a fit Subject thereof ,*

Are diligently handled.

As   alfo the bufinefs of   the   two   Covenants,
wherein is proved that the Covenant of life, is not
made to the feed of Believers, as coming out of
their Loins, and therefore that the baptifm of
Infants is drawn from thence by a falfe Con-
fequence.

By THOMAS PATIENT, a Laborer in the Church
of Chrift at D U B L I N.

Acts 22 16. *And now why tarrieft thou, Arife and be baptized, and wafh away*
thy fins, calling on the name of the Lord. Ephef. 2.12. *Being aliens from the Com-*
mon wealth of Ifrael, and ftrangers to the Covenants of promife. John 3.
5. 6. Jefus anfwered, verily, verily, I fay unto thee, except a man be born of water,
and of the Spirit, he cannot enter into the Kingdom of God; For that which is born
of the flefh is flefh, and that which is born of the fpirit, is fpirit.

London, Printed by *Henry Hills,* and are to be fold at his

houfe at *Sir John Old Caftles in Py-corner* 1654.

BAPTIST HERITAGE

PRESS

www.baptistheritagepress.org

First published 1654
Copyright © 2022 Baptist Heritage Press
All rights reserved.

CONTENTS

THE PARTICULAR CLASSICS SERIES

Series Preface

he *Particular Classics Series* aims to introduce the laity, pastor, and scholar to the classic works of the Particular Baptists. The works included in the series have been carefully selected to both reflect the best of the literature, as well as recover works that have largely been forgotten and/or never republished. It is our hope that these selected works will whet the appetite and summon Baptists to take up and read, to discover our Baptist fathers, and recover a heritage that has been buried for far too long.

One reason I am convinced names like Keach, Collins, Knollys, Coxe, and others do not live on in the hearts of their offspring is because their works are simply inaccessible. If a brave soul does track down a digital scan of one of these books, they will soon discover that it is a product from the Old World, a different world, with odd spellings and long S's that are taxing on modern eyes. The *Particular Classics Series* aims to not only make these works accessible, but aesthetically pleasing and enjoyable to read. These works are apples of gold, and it is a shame if they be not carried in baskets of silver.

To facilitate ease of reading and understanding, the following editorial actions have been made:

1. For uniformity, spelling has been updated to modern standards. For example, words like "satisfie" are changed to "satisfy", "knowledg" to "knowledge", and "ceas'd" to "ceased." While the spelling is updated, *the original wording of the author is still preserved.*

2. Capitalization has been removed from non-proper nouns.

3. Unnecessary italics have been removed. Typically, italics were used in place of quotation marks for Scripture. All italics have been removed and replaced with quotation marks, except for those deemed by the editor to be original to the author's intent of drawing emphasis to a particular word or phrase.

4. Punctuation has been updated to remove excess commas and replace colons and semi-colons with periods or commas where appropriate. At times, the grammar has been slightly modified to better recover the meaning of the author. If a word is missing in the original manuscript so as to make the sentence incomplete (which is not uncommon), the editor has supplied the missing words in brackets ([…]).

5. The original footnotes have been kept. Editorial footnotes are provided in square brackets ([…]) to add more detail to citations, provide uncited Scripture references, or other helpful aid.

6. Paragraph divisions have been made by the editor when deemed necessary to break up a long paragraph. These divisions have been done with care to ensure that units of thought original to the author are kept intact.

7. The original authors used copious amounts of divisions and subdivisions for a topic under consideration. The numerals

employed often become confused, incomplete, or even at times inaccurate. Care has been taken to rectify these errors by using the following gradation of numerals—1, (1), [a], first, and *first*.

8. Chapter and headings have been added to help aid the reader. When possible, these headings are taken by the author himself, but in some cases they have been crafted by the editor to facilitate ease of reading.

9. For uniformity, all quoted Scripture passages conform to the King James Version (matching the 1987 printing), unless it is obvious the original author is working with the Greek and Hebrew to support a point. The Particular Baptists used the Great Bible, the Geneva Bible, and the King James Bible. Those who had university training often examined the Greek and Hebrew.

In all editorial decisions, I have been cautious rather than assertive. Like an archaeologist delicately brushing off the dirt to preserve antiquity buried underneath the surface, so I have sought merely to brush off the dirt rather than shovel carelessly.

To quote Benjamin Keach, "I shall not therefore retain thee longer at the door." Enter the door and see for yourself the grand mansion our Baptist fathers left us. Be no longer an orphan, but come and listen to the voices of the past. In a new age when so many side trails tempt us, continue walking in the ancient paths our brave forefathers have trod before us.

QUINN R. MOSIER
Kansas City, MO
Soli Deo Gloria

THE EPISTLE TO THE
CHRISTIAN READER

*To whom the author wisheth all grace and peace from God the
Father through our Lord Jesus Christ*

here being but a small moment of time from the
Lord allotted to men in this life to run that Christian race set before them, and considering what
Christ saith that whilst it is day we ought to work,
for "the night cometh, when no man can work,"[1] and further
considering that Christ Jesus is gone to fetch a kingdom and to
return, having left his servants several talents to be accounted
for at his coming, when every man's reward or punishment shall
be according to his works,[2] [this] ought to provoke and stir up
every Christian to a conscientious and careful improvement of
his strength for God's glory and the service of his generation in
this pilgrimage.

These, among many other motives, prevailed with me to present this treatise to thy view, being also pressed thereunto by many

---

[1] [John 9:4.]
[2] [cf. Matt. 25:14–30.]

of God's people, formerly in England and of late in Ireland, who have heard me upon the same subject deliver the substance of what is herein contained, both in England and in Ireland.

Beloved reader, I know the world is filled with many books stuffed with very much of man's wisdom, which though the apostle saith is "enmity against God,"[3] yet we find such discourses most pleasing to the carnal hearts of men in our age. Therefore, if that be the thing that thy itching ears do thirst after, thou mayest spare thyself that labour. For thou wilt find that with as much simplicity and plainness as possibly I could I have herein given out, by clear Scripture evidence, what the Lord hath made known to me, for the clearing of this weighty point, which God, by his mighty power, hath subjected my heart to believe, the which formerly by reason of my ignorance and error I was much averse unto.

For after it pleased God to reveal his Son in me and to work a change in my heart, the great and weighty thing that God presented to me was to make my calling and election sure,[4] which I found to be a work filled with many difficulties, considering how far hypocrites might attain in the profession of godliness, and that they might come to have the counterfeit of all the grace in the child of God. And this the rather appeared more difficult because I found my own heart so desperately wicked and full of deceit,[5] and also found the wiles and subtilties of the devil to be various, and I constantly under several temptations and deep desertions when God, though for a little season, withdrew himself

---

[3] [cf. Rom. 8:7.]
[4] [cf. 2 Pet. 1:10.]
[5] Jeremiah 17:9.

and the light of his countenance from me. At which time I judged it my only thing necessary to prove whether Christ were in me and my faith right, as also my sincerity to the Lord. At which time I found but little settled rest or peace till the Lord had put that great question out of doubt in giving me a sure and well-grounded confidence of my interest in him, till which time I found little disposition to search narrowly into other truths which I then thought to be too remote for me to exercise myself in, having received so much spiritual benefit in communing with God and mine own heart, and searching out the difference betwixt the speaking of God's Spirit, my own spirit, and the spirit of Satan.

But when I came to some good measure of settlement in my confident and well-grounded hopes that I was the Lord's, then presently was I tempted, touching the main and material fundamental points in religion. Which temptations, as they were a great cause of trouble and restlessness in my soul, occasioned me with great eagerness, night and day, in use of the best means God presented to me to seek satisfaction in the same. At which time the Lord did carry on my soul with much vehemency after him, so with much unweariedness.

For usually, as one case and weighty question was answered to my satisfaction and comfort, another was stated in my soul too hard for me, in which experiences I, for many years, was exercised with all, in which time I was ignorant of the true way which Christ would have his people to walk in.

But presently, being convinced of the unwarrantableness of the government of the lordly prelates, and the liturgy in the Church of England, and the mixed communions in the parish assemblies, I was resolved, God-willing, to examine all religion, as well in worship and the order of God's house, as I had done in other points. But I, at this time being by the divine power of God converted from the Church of England, though with a great deal of difficulty, was well-furnished with arguments from pulpit and print and divers able disputants for the defense of that false way. But God, breaking in by the power of his Spirit with clear Scripture light, subjected my heart to the obedience of the truth so that I found my heart closing with those truths in the love thereof.

At this time, many godly Christians going to New England, and being come up in my judgment to the way of New England in faith and order, went over thither, being not convinced of my error and great darkness in sprinkling the carnal seed of believers. But verily, I thought I had good warrant for that practise, having then, in substance, the same grounds for the defense thereof that generally, to this day, is urged for the same. Yet, having in my heart so clear a light, discovering how shamefully in many things I had been deluded, and that by those which I could not but have charity to think were the Lord's own servants, and finding the danger of receiving truths by tradition, was resolved to examine that point of baptism. And so, I constantly resorted to the meetings of the people in New England, desiring to have good satisfaction in them and their doctrine and practice before I joined in communion.

In order, thereunto, I constantly attended the preaching of the word, where hearing many often preaching for baptizing of children of believing parents, I began to examine the grounds thereof, and the weight of their arguments and genuine scope and drift of the Scriptures alleged by them to prove that point. I found that the Scriptures were being generally wrested and abused contrary to their native tendency and proper drift and scope. I also found, as I conceived, the foundation argument they urged was so exceeding contrary to several foundations of religion, which both they and I did believe.

These things being hinted into my soul, I was resolved to examine the same as I had formerly with great profit and advantage in several other points of religion. But upon this resolution, temptations came in upon my heart that I was but weak. And in case it were not a truth, did I think so many men eminent for religion, piety, gifts, and parts should not discover it sooner than I? Therefore, it was to no purpose for me to trouble myself. Unto which I had this answer in my soul: that I had been too long misled already on that ground, submitting to the liturgy and that corrupt hierarchy.

Again, I considered that when the angels came with that message of glad tidings to all people in Luke the second chapter, declaring the birth and nativity of Christ, the Lord then made the choice of the poor simple shepherds watching their flocks by night.

In the first place, this eminent truth was delivered and revealed to them when all the learned and eminent men in Israel had no knowledge thereof.

And finding the poor thief on the cross to have a sounder judgement than the general synod or council of learned men at Jerusalem, and also the speech of Christ to this purpose in

Matthew 11:25, where Christ thanks his Father for hiding these things from the wise and prudent and revealing them to babes and sucklings out of his good pleasure, the Spirit, being like the wind, which bloweth when and where it listeth.[6]

And also, finding some of Christ's disciples bearing testimony of Christ in Luke 19:38–40, the Pharisees desired Christ to rebuke them. But Christ answered and said, "I tell you that, if these should hold their peace, the stones would immediately cry out." Where, I observed, Christ to descend and not to ascend; he doth not say if his simple and weak disciples should neglect their testimony learned Pharisees would cry out, but if his disciples neglect, the stones should, which manifests that God loves to choose the most simple and foolish things to reveal his will by.

And then again I found God had not so much engaged, by promise, to reveal himself to men considered of such outward and excellent parts, but in Psalm 25:14, "The secret of the LORD is with them that fear him; and he will shew them his covenant." And Christ saith in John 15:14–15, "Ye are my friends, if ye do whatsoever I command you. Henceforth I call you not servants; for the servant knoweth not what his Lord doeth: but I have called you friends; for all things that I have heard of my Father I have made known unto you." And David saith, "Thou hast made me wiser than my teachers, because I have kept thy commandments."[7] Where, the Lord promises teaching principally to such as fear him and conscientiously keep his commandments, guid-

---

[6] [cf. John 3:8.]

[7] [Patient does not list a scripture citation here, but seems to be quoting Psalm 119:99. However, his wording does not match the verse in totality. "I have more understanding than all my teachers: for thy testimonies are my meditation."]

ing them in judgment, and in the way that he should choose.

Notwithstanding, I found further objections in my heart, that though it was not men of parts and outward learning, but babes and sucklings having their hearts bowed to obedience and to the holy fear of God that God would teach, yet I was sensible of so much evil in my heart that I questioned whether I might not be misled. Upon which I was put upon humble and fervent prayers to the Lord to guide and teach me, and to reveal his mind to me, having again resolutions to seek the mind of God in this truth, and great encouragements to believe that God would satisfy me, and the rather from my former experience of his goodness having satisfied me in many weighty points that I was every way as much unsettled in.

Upon which this temptation came in afresh upon me: what need I trouble myself in a point so disputable? For if by my search and trial in that matter I should come to see grounds swaying in conscience against children's baptism, that then I should be generally despised and slighted of all the godly in that country, and not only be frustrated of communion and fellowship with them, but must expect to suffer imprisonment, confiscation of goods, and banishment at least, which would be my ruin, not knowing where to go but in the woods amongst Indians and wild beasts.

Under this temptation I had a sore conflict. My evil and treacherous heart resisted the blessed motions of the Spirit of God, but considered that the ground of these discouraging arguments did arise from the flesh and the devil, as Peter when he said, "Pity thyself, Master, this thing shall not be to thee."[8] My res-

---

[8] [Patient's quotation from Matthew 16:22 is a paraphrase, or embellishment, on the text.]

olution was, as Christ saith, "Get thee behind me, Satan…thou savourest not the things that be of God."[9]

Which put me in no small agony or conflict for some good space together. But it pleased the Lord to set that Scripture home upon my heart, "Buy the truth, and sell it not."[10] Buy the truth at any rate, but sell it at no rate. If truth cost me my life, I must buy it. Though I might have all the favour and friendship in the world, I must not sell it. This wrought in me a grounded and settled resolution that I would seek after the mind of God, as well in suffering truths as other, because Christ saith, "He that keeps the word of my patience, I also will keep him in the hour of temptation."[11] Apprehending that to be the words of Christ's patience, he embracing and practicing whereof would bring the cross, that is, contempt and hatred from all sorts of men, I found Christ said for this cause he was born and came into the world: to bear witness to the truth.[12] These things satisfied me, and that from the Lord, that I ought to make diligent search what his mind was in this point.

Hereupon, I found the special presence of God with me, carrying out my heart to the Lord by faith and earnest prayer to be instructed and guided, all which time I was not acquainted with any that opposed christening children, and conversed only with such as were for that practice. I found my carnal part to desire satisfaction in infant baptism, but the more I conferred with or heard any preach for it, the more was I convinced of the folly

[9] [Matt. 16:23.]
[10] [Prov. 23:23.]
[11] [Rev. 3:10.]
[12] [John 18:37.]

xii

and ignorance of that judgment and practice, having heard one man preach fifteen sermons upon this subject, urging that in substance which many considerable authors had wrote.

I also searched many authors who wrote thereof night and day with much attention, weighing and examining the grounds they urged, many times breaking my sleep by watching in the night season. At the last, it pleased the Lord to reveal his mind to me so that I was enlightened in my understanding to see answers to whatsoever I had heard. The Lord broke in with not only a clear light in me as to the matter in question, but three days, one after another, coming into my soul with sealing manifestations of his love and that with such Scriptures so pertinent and suitable to my condition.

At this time, there was a warrant issued out to apprehend and bring me before the general court in New England, which was no trouble to me, being filled with unspeakable joy as I walked up and down in the woods in that wilderness about my business. And this discovery from God did much settle me in that truth, which in substance thou wilt find in this treatise. Upon which, God wrought in me a true repentance and sorrow of heart that I had so long, both in opinion and practice, gone in so sinful a way as I found that to be.

I have not, in this treatise, gone about to undertake a confutation of any one man, but upon my long experience in this subject matter have taken up the main argument, which is the foundation that all the rest are grounded upon, and have bent my understanding in answer to that which being overthrown all other arguments fall with it.

Christian reader, I judge the clear evidence of Scripture light, which I do here give out to confirm the dipping [of] believers, will be sufficient to reprove all that darkness generally asserted in many large discourses about this point of christening of children.

But further, that which I have had much in observation hath been a great deal of malice and contempt discovered from the devil against this truth.

First, in that the devil did, by his subtilties and fair pretenses in the first apostacy, sow this error in the minds of people that this ordinance was of use to regenerate and convey grace. And then, who should be thought unfit to receive it; it had been a great unmercifulness to let children or any be without the same.

Thus, that subtle enemy, the devil, destroys God's ordinances and sets up another of his own in the room thereof, which still remains upon the Papists, and generally all our carnal Protestants, both priests and people, concluding the dangerous estate of that child that dies unbaptized. Therefore, midwives on this ground were tolerated to baptize if a child were like to die, putting such a value thereon as if it had conveyed grace.

But many good men have renounced this, though the devil hath shewed his malice in blinding them still to practice the same evil, though upon another ground, lately found out, and that is the subject this book opposeth. Others see the darkness and error of christening carnal children upon any ground, but the devil shews his rage against that ordinance in them that rather than they will embrace it as from the Lord, contradict and oppose the same, saying, "There is no ordinance or church to be found in the world." His malice also appears in such as boast of their being above ordinances, saying that Christ and ordinances are at [an] end, that dispensation being for that time or age; but now they have Christ in Spirit, the substance being come, the shadows vanish.

Thus, the devil strangely appears like himself, as if he had forgot his language in the Papist and carnal Protestant that this ordinance regenerated in the very work done, and that the salvation or damnation depended upon it, when, now in others, what is washing or dipping in a little water, but a low or legal thing? So that if the devil's delusions and inventions are not closed withal, then Christ's ordinances are vilified and contemned.

And further, Satan manifests his malice in throwing contempt upon the obedient and upright practisers of the same, to raise prejudices from a story of what strange creatures were of that opinion at Münster in Germany,[13] and stirs up others to pry into the dark side of the saints; I mean their personal frailties as the Egyptians in the Red Sea, to their own destructions. The cloud was darkness to them, but gave light to the Israelites.[14] The Egyptians' eyes were only on the black, or dark side of the cloud. Therefore, they stumbled and fell, but the Israelites had the light part thereof for their safety, which is compared to the conversation of the saints where there is a light part, their graces and virtues, but their dark part is their failings, which malice or prejudice will not suffer many men to see beyond.[15] For a man that

---

[13] [Patient is referencing the Münster rebellion in 1534-1535, when radical Anabaptists took over the city of Münster, attempting to establish a communal sectarian government.]

[14] Exod. 14:20.

[15] Heb. 12:1.

hates his brother walks in darkness, as John saith.[16] The tempter accused Job that he did not serve God for nought; he was hedged about.[17] God had preferred him to honour and riches and place of authority in the world, as appears in Job 29, which malice he nowadays manifesteth against the prosperity of his saints, desiring to stain their holy obedience with improbrious language of self-seeking and preferment, when the professors of this truth have been the persons ordinarily stoned and suffering the violence of the multitudes, where they have not been protected by godly magistrates.

Christian friend, do not read this book with a heart prejudiced against the same for the sake of the instrument, or plainness of the style. It was not intended to please men, but in faithfulness to discharge a duty to God, from whom I received what I have laid before thee, and to answer the call of many Christians which have been, for some years, past neglected through my indisposedness to this work. However, if thou shalt, by this my weak endeavour, reap any satisfaction or edification in the truth, let God, the author of every good and perfect gift, have the praise, which is only due to him and not to his,

Unworthy Servant,
THOMAS PATIENT

---

[16] [cf. 1 Jn. 2:9, 11.]
[17] [cf. Job 1:9–10.]

Baptism and the Distinction of the Covenants

1

The Ordinance of Baptism Explained

Now when they heard this, they were pricked in their heart, and said unto Peter and to the rest of the apostles, Men and brethren, what shall we do? Then Peter said unto them, Repent, and be baptized every one of you in the name of Jesus Christ for the remission of sins, and ye shall receive the gift of the Holy Ghost.

Acts 2:37–38

hese words of my text have a special dependence upon the words foregoing in the chapter, for in the beginning of the chapter you shall find that the apostles and the church were all, with one accord, in one place when the day of Pentecost was fully come. And according to the promise that Jesus Christ commanded them to wait for, and that John had foretold of, that one should come after him that should baptize with the Holy Ghost and with fire, the which was at this time fulfilled.[1] For as the author of Acts here relates,

Suddenly there came a sound from heaven as of a rushing

---

[1] [cf. Matt. 3:11; Luke 3:16.]

mighty wind, and it filled all the house where they were sitting. And there appeared unto them cloven tongues like as of fire, and it sat upon each of them. And they were all filled with the Holy Ghost, and began to speak with other tongues, as the Spirit gave them utterance.[2]

Now this I understand to be the baptism which John speaks of, namely, that of the Holy Ghost and of fire, which Christ should dispense, as you may see was extraordinary and upon special occasion communicated to the apostles, they being now to give testimony of Christ's death, resurrection, and ascension. The Lord, in order to this work, communicates to them the extraordinary gifts of the Holy Ghost, and that in an extraordinary manner. For here was outward signs which were cloven tongues of fire resting on them, and here was also the Holy Ghost with the extraordinary effects of it, as the inward things signified by the outward sign, all which was, I understand, extraordinary for the fitting of these apostles to that extraordinary work which God had to do by them.

First, they were to be eyewitnesses of Christ's majesty in the flesh.

Secondly, they were to be master-builders to lay a foundation, which all after ministers, to the end of the world, were to build on, they being [the] penmen of Scripture.

Thirdly, they were now to overthrow all the Jewish worship and all the mosaical administrations put to an end by Christ's death, and to furnish them to this extraordinary work, which Christ, as an effect of his session at the right hand of God, pours

---

[2] [Acts 2:2–4.]

2

down these gifts upon them, as beforementioned. This being noised abroad, how they spake with other tongues, the multitude came together wondering at them, and some thought they had been drunk. But Peter, standing up with the eleven, began to lift up his voice to teach them.

And first, he proves by Scripture that these gifts of the Holy Ghost were formerly promised by the Lord, and as an effect of his ascension now given to them. And he endeavours in this sermon preached to prove,

First, that Jesus was the Christ, a man approved of God by miracles and signs that God did work by him amongst them.

Secondly, he endeavours to prove by Scripture that he did suffer and die according to the counsel and will of God.

Thirdly, that he did rise again from the dead, which he from Scripture doth justify.

Fourthly, that God had exalted him by his right hand to be both Lord and Christ.[3] And he proves that by the visible gifts of the Holy Ghost, which they did see and hear. And lest they should not understand who he meant, he tells them in the verse before my text that it was that same Jesus which they had crucified that God had made "both Lord and Christ."

"Now when they heard this, they were pricked in their hearts, and said unto Peter and to the rest of the apostles, Men and brethren, what shall we do?"[4]

Whence observe from the text that preaching and hearing the gospel preached is a special means to convert souls, as appears

---

[3] [cf. Acts 2:36.]

[4] [Acts 2:37.]

3

when Peter preached and clearly held forth that he whom they had crucified and slain was now to be Lord and judge, and exalted to that dignity by God the Father. When they heard this, they were pricked in their hearts.

In the second place, we may observe from hence that true conversion begins with a prick in the heart.

Thirdly, they, when wrought upon and pricked in their hearts, "said to Peter and to the rest of the apostles, Men and brethren, what shall we do?"

Whence in the third place, observe that it is the disposition of such that have the beginning of saving light to desire more, and that from them whom God hath spoken to their souls by.

Fourthly, that which they do earnestly inquire after is: what shall we do? Which respects obedience. They, believing Christ to be a Lord as well as a Saviour, know that he must be submitted to. Therefore, said they, "What shall we do?" Whence we observe that a true converted soul is an obedient soul.

In verse 38, the answer of Peter to them is in these words, "Repent, and be baptized every one of you." From whence, we do observe further that where the gospel is preached, all men are called to repent.

Lastly, that it is the duty of every man that believes and repents to be baptized.

Now this last observation of the text is that which I shall at present speak to for the satisfaction of such souls that may, at present, be doubtful of this truth, and for the confirming such souls as do already believe it.

Now for the better and more clear speaking to this point in

hand, I shall explain what this ordinance of baptism is, and that in four things which will more clearly appear if we examine the commission that Christ gives his disciples in Matthew 28:19–20, where we find that the eleven disciples were sent by Christ, who hath all power in heaven and earth given to him. Christ saith, "Go ye therefore, and teach all nations, baptizing them in the name of the Father, and of the Son, and of the Holy Ghost: Teaching them to observe all things whatsoever I have commanded you." From whence you may observe four things contained in this commission essential to this ordinance of baptism. Here is first the ministry, secondly the form, thirdly the name into which, and fourthly the subjects.

I. WHO A LAWFUL MINISTER OF BAPTISM IS

First, the ministers that must dispense this ordinance, and that is preaching disciples. And so, in the 16th verse are the eleven denominated. Then the eleven disciples went away into Galilee, and Jesus, in verse 18, came and spake unto them, saying, "All power is given unto me in heaven and earth. Go ye therefore, and teach all nations, baptizing them." Whence you may observe, that the persons bid to go are disciples enabled to teach the doctrine of the gospel for the conversion of souls to faith and repentance. For it is clear that *they that are bid to teach are bid to baptize also.* So that from this commission I gather that a disciple enabled to bring down God to a soul and to bring a soul again up to God is a lawful minister of baptism. For that is the tenor of the new covenant. "I will be to them a God, and they shall be to me a peo-

5

ple" and "I am my beloved's, and my beloved is mine."[5] So that, as God in Christ is to be opened, and that in all the fundamental doctrines of faith for man's salvation, so is the soul's conformity to God to be preached as the soul's duty to God again. So that where God hath furnished a minister with abilities from himself to declare the doctrine of faith and repentance to conversion, and having converted that soul is furnished with the knowledge of God to teach to this soul all the fundamental ordinances, according to the commission which saith, "Teaching them to observe all things whatsoever I have commanded you,"[6] it is, without doubt, that this is a justifiable minister sent from the Lord according to the commission. But though a man should be able to preach the doctrine of faith, and that ably for the conversion of souls unto that faith, yet being destitute of the true knowledge of the doctrine of baptism, and how it ought to be dispensed, to be sure, this man is not a justifiable minister according to the commission because he is ignorant of his commission, that when he hath converted souls to the faith, neither knows how to discover to these men the fundamental ordinances of God, neither can discover to them the evil of those superstitious practices, which they have been nursed up in by the traditions of their fathers.

Yet notwithstanding, I dare not say, but so far as they have a gift they are warranted to administer the same from 1 Peter 4:10, who saith, "Let everyone as he hath received the gift minister."[7] And so, it was lawful for any Christian man, in that sense, to ad-

---

[5] Heb. 8:10; Cant. 6:3.

[6] [Matt. 28:20.]

[7] [Patient's quotation of 1 Peter 4:10 differs from the KJV, which reads, "As every man hath received the gift, even so minister the same one to another, as good stewards of the manifold grace of God."]

minister such gifts which God hath bestowed on them.

But sure it is that these that are utterly unacquainted how to dispense the ordinance of baptism were never sent of God to dispense it, that instead of dipping do sprinkle, and instead of the true subject, *a believer,* dispense it upon a carnal ignorant child. And instead of doing it into the name of Father, Son, and Holy Ghost, do sprinkle them at the naming of so many words only.

II. THE TRUE FORM OF BAPTISM

In the second place, the true form of baptism is commanded of the Lord Jesus by way of dipping, and, as it were, by drowning, overwhelming, or burying in water, and not by sprinkling with water, as appears many ways.

First, in that although there be frequent mention made of that appointment of Christ in his last will and testament, yet it is never expressed in the word that may be rendered *rantism* or *sprinkling,* but by the word that is rendered *baptism* or *dipping.*

Secondly, in that the word by which it is so frequently expressed doth, in proper English, signify to dip, to plunge under water, and, as it were, to drown them so as with safety the party, as to the manner, may be drowned again and again.

See the instance of Naaman who dipped himself seven times in Jordan.[8] To this sense of the word, at least in this place, both the Greek, Latin, and English churches agree, as is affirmed by able authors.

Thirdly, in that the phrase in which there is mention made of such an appointment of Christ is affirmed doth necessarily

[8] 2 Kgs. 5:14.

import such a thing. And, therefore, when mention is made of baptizing, which is commonly translated *in* or *into*, suits with dipping, and not that preposition which signifies *with*, and so suits with sprinkling.

And, therefore, it may be as well rendered, "I baptize you *in* water, and he shall baptize you *in* the Holy Spirit."[9] So it is rendered, "John did baptize *in* the wilderness" and "*in* the river of Jordan."[10] Or that John was *in* the Spirit on the Lord's Day.[11] And they were baptized *in* the cloud and *in* the sea.[12] It may as well be rendered, "I baptize you, or dip you, *into* water," as it is rendered, they were "casting a net *into* the sea," for which the words are affirmed to be the same.[13] And it would be too improper a speech to say John did baptize *with* the wilderness, and they were casting a net *with* the sea.

Fourthly, that this appointment of Christ is by way of dipping and not sprinkling appears in that for the resemblance and likeness hereunto the Israelites [who passed] under the cloud and in the sea, where the Egyptians—that were their lords and commanders, their pursuers and enemies, that sought their destruction—were drowned, left behind, and seen no more, is, by the Holy Spirit, called a baptism.[14] They were baptized "in the cloud."

Where observe, it is not here rendered *with* the cloud and *with* the sea, as in the other place *with* water, because it suits

---

[9] Mark 1:8.
[10] Mark 1:4–5. [Emphasis added by Patient.]
[11] Rev. 1:10.
[12] 1 Cor. 10:2.
[13] Mark 1:16.
[14] 1 Cor. 10:2.

with sprinkling, although the word be the same,[15] but *in* the cloud and *in* the sea, which suits with dipping or overwhelming, and so with the appointment of Christ. They, passing through the midst of the Red, or bloody, Sea on dry land, which stood on both sides as a wall, and being under the cloud as men, in a carnal eye, overwhelmed and drowned, and yet truly saved and safe from their enemies.

Fifthly, that this appointment of Christ was not by sprinkling but by dipping or putting the person into or under water appears by Philip baptizing the Eunuch. It is said they went both down into the water, both Philip, the baptizer, and the eunuch, the person to be baptized. And being there in the water, Philip baptized, or dipped, him in that water as John did Jesus in the river of Jordan.

And it is said they descended, or went down, into the water, so they ascended, or went straight way up, or out of the water.[16] Mark the expression, "And Jesus, when he was baptized, went up straightway out of the water."[17] Therefore, he had been down in the water.

Sixthly, that this appointment of Christ was not by sprinkling but by dipping, or as it were a drowning, appears in that John the Baptizer, his work being to baptize, remains in the wilderness by the river of Jordan, and afterwards in Aenon, near Salim.[18] And the reason that is rendered by the Spirit of the Lord why he abode there was because there was much water, which need not have

---

[15] Mark 1:8.

[16] See for this Acts 8:38–39; Matt. 3:16.

[17] [Matt. 3:16.]

[18] [John 3:23.]

been if that appointment could have been performed by sprinkling and not by dipping.[19]

Seventhly, that this appointment of Christ was not to be performed by sprinkling but by dipping appears from the nature of the ordinance itself. For it is such an ordinance as whereby the person that submitteth thereto doth visibly put on Christ Jesus the Lord and is hereby visibly planted into his death, holding forth therein a lively similitude and likeness unto his death, whereby only through faith he now professeth he hath escaped death and is in hopes to obtain life everlasting, and so to have fellowship with him in his death and to reckon himself dead with him to sin, Satan, the law, and the curse.[20] But the planting of a person into the likeness of death is no way resembled by sprinkling, but by dipping it is lively set forth and demonstrated.

Eighthly, this appointment of Christ's baptism is an ordinance whereby the person that submitteth thereto doth hereby visibly and clearly resemble the burial of Christ and his being buried in respect of the old man, the former lusts and corruptions, like the Egyptians, to be taken away and seen no more.[21] But sprinkling doth no way lively resemble the burial of Christ, or the person being buried with him as dipping doth.

Ninthly, this appointment of Christ's baptism is an ordinance whereby the person that submitteth thereto doth visibly and lively hold forth herein the resurrection of Christ, declares him whose life was taken away from the earth to be alive again, who although he died and was buried, yet was not left in the grave to

---

[19] See Luke 3:2–3; John 3:23.
[20] See Gal. 3:27; Rom. 6:2–3, 5, 7, 9; 1 Cor. 15:29.
[21] Rom. 6:4, 6; Col. 2:12.

see corruption, but was raised again and, behold, he liveth forevermore.

And as hereby he holds forth the resurrection of Christ, so doth he also his own, being planted in the likeness thereof so as to reckon himself to be, in soul and spirit, quickened and risen with Christ from henceforth to live unto God, the fountain of life, and Christ Jesus the Lord, who died for him and rose again, and so to walk in newness of life in this present world, being also begot into a lively hope, that in the world to come he shall be raised and quickened both in soul and body to a life everlasting.[22] But sprinkling doth [in] no way lively resemble the resurrection of Christ, or the soul, or bodies rising, or being raised by him as the way of dipping doth.

Therefore, this appointment of Christ was, and still is, to be performed by way of dipping or putting the person into, or under, the water, and not by sprinkling.

Tenthly, dipping doth hold forth a conformity to Christ in his sufferings and afflictions, as Christ saith, "I have a baptism…and how am I straitened till it be accomplished," meaning his sufferings.[23]

Now one end of baptism is to represent Christ's sufferings and our sufferings with him, which is in a lively manner set out by dipping into water. And therefore, when the saints do express their afflictions, they do set them forth by being in the depths, or in the deep waters, as David in Psalm 130:1, "Out of the depths have I cried unto thee, O LORD," meaning deep afflictions. And

---

[22] See Rom. 6:4, 5, 8, 11; Acts 8:33, 35–36; Col. 2:12; 1 Cor. 15:29; 1 Pet. 1:3.
[23] [Luke 12:50.]

11

God saith in Isaiah 43:2, "When thou passest through the waters…they shall not overflow thee," meaning affliction.

And therefore, a believer is to be dipped and plunged all over into the river, or water, to hold forth that now he must resolve to take up the cross of Christ and suffer. And not only so, but this being raised and delivered out of the water again by the hands of the minister doth hold forth that so shall such believing souls be saved and delivered from all their afflictions, as in Psalm 34:19, "Many are the afflictions of the righteous: but the LORD delivereth him out of them all."

And that this doth sign, or signify, our salvation appears in 1 Peter 3:21, the like figure whereunto "baptism doth also now save us" and Mark 16:16, "He that believeth and is baptized shall be saved." So that baptism is to sign and confirm signally our sufferings and afflictions with Christ, so salvation or deliverance from them all—the one in dipping and plunging him in water, the other in raising him out again.

III. INTO WHOSE NAME BAPTISM IS ADMINISTERED

The third thing that is essential in this ordinance of baptism, which I shall speak to, will be what is meant by name of Father, Son, and Holy Ghost. The command is that the minister must dip them into the name of the Father, Son, and Holy Ghost, the which the Lord Jesus commanding must be therefore essential to this ordinance. I shall, therefore, endeavour to shew you what is meant by name here.

That by which Father, Son, and Spirit are made known, as a man is by his name, that is hereto be understood by the name

Father, Son, and Holy Ghost. We know the gospel doth hold forth one God, yet distinguished into Father, Son, and Holy Ghost. The name here is to be understood that gospel that doth so set forth God and describe him as the subject matter of our faith. "But the Lord said unto him [Ananias], Go thy way: for he is a chosen vessel unto me, to bear my name before the Gentiles, and kings, and the children of Israel: For I will shew him how great things he must suffer for my name's sake."[24]

Now *name* in this place, and in the commission, is to be understood that heavenly mystery of the gospel in which God is discovered and made known as a man by his name.

One part of the gospel mystery consists of a discovery of the name of the Father, by which he is distinguishably made known from the Son and Spirit, and that in these particulars.

First, in ordaining the Son,[25] in choosing and electing the Son,[26] in sending the Son,[27] in sealing the Son,[28] in promising the Son,[29] in bruising the Son and putting him to grief,[30] and laying all our iniquities upon the Son, and to justify and freely accept such as believe in the Son. This I understand is the name of the Father.

And by the Son's name is to be understood that by which he makes known himself to the sons and daughters of men as to

---

[24] Acts 9:15–16.

[25] 1 Pet. 1:18. [Patient might have meant to cite 1 Peter 1:20.]

[26] Isa. 28:16; 1 Pet. 2:5.

[27] Gal. 4:4; John 3:16–17.

[28] John 6:27.

[29] Isa. 9:6.

[30] Isa. 53.

take flesh.[31] He kept the law in order to die as that just one, or as a lamb without spot, and his making his soul an offering for sin as a perfect offering for the sins and transgressions of his people,[32] and that he did not only die for our sins, but rose again for our justification,[33] and ascended into heaven and makes intercession for us,[34] and pours down the Spirit and gives gifts unto men.[35] All this the Son makes himself known by as by a name distinguishably from the Father, and the Spirit.

And in the last place, the Spirit is made known in the gospel as that which in the first place convinceth the world of sin,[36] and pricks men in their hearts with a sense of sin and the wrath of God due for sin.[37] And the work of the Spirit, by which that is made known, is the revealing of the Father and the Son and those great mysteries unto the soul of a poor convicted sinner. For as Christ saith, the Spirit of God shall lead you into all truth, it shall take of mine, and shew it to you.[38] And so, no man doth understand the things of a man, but the spirit of a man that is within him. So none shall or can understand the things of God, but by the Spirit of God.[39] "For the Spirit of God searcheth out all things, yea, even the deep things of God."[40] The Spirit doth not only discover man's misery and his lost estate by reason of sin, but dis-

---

[31] Heb. 2:14; Rom. 1:3; 9:5.
[32] Heb. 10:12, 14; Isa. 53.
[33] Rom. 4:25.
[34] Heb. 7:25. [cf. Rom. 8:34.]
[35] Zech. 12:10; Eph. 4:10–12.
[36] John 16:8.
[37] Acts 2:37.
[38] John 16. [esp. 16:13–14.]
[39] [1 Cor. 2:11.]
[40] 1 Cor. 2:9–10.

covers a remedy which lies in the great love of God in Christ, as before mentioned, and worketh in the heart true faith and repentance, disposing the heart to obedience. This is the proper work or office of the Spirit by which he is distinguishably known from the Father and the Son.

And now, when the soul shall come to the preacher and make known to him that [which] the Spirit hath experimentally made known unto him, his lost and damnable estate by sin, and that the same Spirit hath discovered unto him the great love of God the Father in the gift of Christ to be a propitiation for sin as one dying for the chief of sinners, and that the Spirit of God hath made known all this to him and hath wrought faith in his heart to believe it, and hath changed his heart from a course of sin to renewed obedience. For no soul can declare to a minister the true work of conversion. But he must, in so doing, discover his knowledge of the work of the Father, Son, and Spirit. And into this doth the minister baptize him as in the name of the Father, Son, and Holy Ghost. And thus much for these three particulars.

IV. THE SUBJECT OF BAPTISM

In the fourth place, we shall now come to the subject that must be baptized, and that, as you have heard, is one that is taught. "Teach all nations, baptizing them."[41] And as my text saith, "Repent, and be baptized every one of you," which doth hold forth the person baptized to be a taught and repentant person.[42]

But seeing the main thing in question hath always seemed

---

[41] [Matt. 28:19.]

[42] [Acts 2:38.]

15

to be the subject of baptism, who it is that is to be baptized, this I shall therefore most insist upon, wherein I shall endeavour to make plain to you first, as I say, that he is to be a believer, a penitent person, as appears Mark 16:15–16, "Go ye into all the world, and preach the gospel to every creature. He that believeth and is baptized shall be saved." Where observe that believing the gospel is to go before baptizing. "Teach all nations, baptizing" or "dipping them".[43] What *them*? Them that are taught or made disciples by teaching.

And in my text you find that Peter, after Christ had poured down the Spirit upon them, doth by that authority received from heaven, when he had converted those Jews, command every one of them to be baptized, or dipped. "Repent, and be baptized every one of you in the name of Jesus Christ for the remission of sins."[44] And so, in like manner you shall find Cornelius and his family by Peter commanded to be baptized. For saith he to the six brethren that were with him, "Can any man forbid water, that these should not be baptized, which have received the Holy Ghost as well as we?"[45]

And he, by the great authority which, as an extraordinary apostle, he had from heaven, commanded them to be baptized in the name of the Lord Jesus. So we find Ananias, in a special manner, sent to the apostle Paul at his first conversion to the faith, as Acts 22:16 where he also, by the authority received from Christ, in verse the 16th saith, "And now [Paul] why tarriest thou? arise, and be baptized, and wash away thy sins, calling on the name of

---

[43] Matt. 28:19.
[44] [Acts 2:38.]
[45] Acts 10:47–48

the Lord," where you see the express command of God enjoining him, upon his conversion, to be baptized.

And in the next place, as God hath commanded his ministers to baptize or dip believers only, and as his ministers, by virtue of that authority from him, have left standing laws and commands upon disciples only to be baptized, so we find that they did practice that way, and that only of baptizing such as believed and repented. "Then they that gladly received his word were baptized: and the same day there were added unto them about three thousand souls. And they continued stedfastly in the apostles' doctrine and fellowship, and in breaking of bread, and in prayers."[46] Whence you may observe the practice of the apostles that were guided by the infallible gifts of the Spirit, that first they converted before they baptized.

In like manner, you shall find in Acts 8:12–13 where Philip was preaching to the people in Samaria,

> but when they believed Philip preaching the things concerning the kingdom of God, and the name of Jesus Christ, they were baptized, both men and women. Then Simon himself believed also: and when he was baptized, he continued with Philip, and wondered.

So that you see this was the continued course of Christ's messengers sent by him.

First, they converted men by preaching, and then baptized them in the name of the Father, Son, and Holy Ghost, or in the name of the Lord Jesus, wherein the name of the Father and Spirit are included when his name is only mentioned. In like manner,

---

[46] Acts 2:40–42.

17

you shall find in the same chapter that Philip, by the Spirit of the Lord, being directed to the eunuch that did belong to Candace, the Queen of the Ethiopians, who had the charge of all her treasure and had been at Jerusalem for to worship, was returning and reading Isaiah the prophet. Then, Philip joined himself to his chariot, and upon some discourse together, he, from the aforesaid Scripture, preached unto him Jesus in Acts 8:32, etc.,

> And as they went on their way, they came unto a certain water: and the eunuch said, See, here is water; what doth hinder me to be baptized? And Philip said, If thou believest with all thine heart, thou mayest. And he answered and said, I believe that Jesus Christ is the Son of God. And he commanded the chariot to stand still: and they went down both into the water, both Philip and the eunuch; and he baptized him. And when they were come up out of the water, the Spirit of the Lord caught away Philip, that the eunuch saw him no more: and he went on his way rejoicing.[47]

From all these words you may observe that Philip is said to preach Christ unto this man, and upon his coming to the water he said, "What lets?" Where you see, it is the duty of such as believe to offer themselves to be baptized, and that there is no "let" or hinderance to the ordinance of baptism but unbelief. And therefore, saith he, "If thou believest with all thine heart, thou mayest," or "it is lawful," as the word more properly may be read,[48] plainly holding forth that all, both young and old, that did not believe, it was unlawful for them to be baptized.

[47] [Acts 8:36–39.]
[48] [Acts 8:37.]

18

And you shall find several families also baptized upon their being converted, which many, through ignorance and want of taking notice of what the Scripture speaks, say it is probable they had some infants in them.

But to prevent mistakes in the minds of any that so think, I shall prove that these families were all converted disciples so as to believe the gospel. As for instance, first, the family of Lydia.

> And a certain woman named Lydia, a seller of purple, of the city of Thyatira, which worshipped God, heard us: whose heart the Lord opened, that she attended unto the things which were spoken of Paul. And when she was baptized, and her household, she besought us, saying, If ye have judged me to be faithful to the Lord, come into my house, and abide there. And she constrained us.[49]

Now here, in this text, Lydia is only mentioned as to have been converted; no mention [is] made what her household was, only that they were baptized. But in the last verse, namely, the 40th of that chapter, it is said that when Paul and Silas were put out of the jailer's house, they went and "entered into the house of Lydia: and when they had seen the brethren, they comforted them, and departed." Where you may clearly see that Lydia's house consisted of brethren capable of being visited and comforted by Paul and Silas, as well as Lydia whose household they were.

And also, in the same chapter you have mention made of the jailer and his household, all which were baptized in verses 31–34, in which place you shall, upon reading, find this to be true, that they spake unto him the word of the Lord and to all that were in

---

[49] Acts 16:14–15.

19

his house. And verse 34, "He set meat before them, and rejoiced, believing in God with all his house." Where it is plain that the whole household of the jailer heard the word of God and rejoiced and believed, as well as the jailer, and were all baptized, which is a clear proof that such hearing the word of God and believing ought, and they only, to be baptized.

And this will appear further by the house of Stephanus, comparing 1 Corinthians 1:16 with 1 Corinthians 16:15–16, where in the one place it is said that Paul baptized the household of Stephanus. In the last place, he speaketh thus, "Now I urge you, brothers—you know that the household of Stephanas were the first converts in Achaia, and that they have devoted themselves to the service of the saints—be subject to such as these, and to every fellow worker and laborer."

Where you see in one and the same epistle, as he saith, he baptizeth this household, so he affirms they were the firstfruits of Achaia, and that they were ministers, and added themselves to the ministering unto saints. They did, as the text notes, labour, and he would have the church submit themselves unto such. Therefore, they were not babes or little infants, but all true converts, believing and penitent persons.

And in Acts 18:8, for the further clearing of this matter in hand, "And Crispus, the chief ruler of the synagogue, believed on the Lord with all his house; and many of the Corinthians hearing believed, and were baptized." So that you see what a catalogue of clear examples you have to confirm unto us, which way those infallible apostles both taught and practiced, according to the great commission given them by the authority of Christ from heaven to preach first the gospel to every creature, and he that believeth and is baptized should be saved, and that they should make disciples through teaching, dipping them into the name of the Father, Son, and Holy Ghost. And withal, you see both commands, as you have heard and plentiful examples for baptizing believers, but not the least colour or shew of any ground for sprinkling of infants.

Now, by the way, let me say what a sad thing, therefore, is this that such a world of people, from custom and tradition, run headlong after this idol of man's invention.

But this solemn ordinance, which you have heard lies clearly as a duty under the express law of Christ to everyone that believeth, this they sleight and condemn as enemies to the same. Therefore, let such souls know that as Christ is a king, so this is one of his great laws and a fundamental ordinance of the gospel unto which he calls all believing and penitent persons that are professed subjects to him to be obedient to.

Now therefore, let such tender souls who have the fear of God in them lay this to heart.

First, that this solemn ordinance, for many hundred years, hath been neither preached nor practised by abundance of such, which in charity we cannot but judge might have many good things found in them.

But here lies that which makes the case sad and lamentable, that in the room of this precious ordinance of God, which Christ confirmed by his blood, should be set up that idol of sprinkling of carnal poor infants. For doubtless, if there be an idol now practised in the world or set up amongst men, this must needs be one.

21

For I have learned, with others of the saints of God, this to be an idol, either the worshipping of a false god or the true God in a false manner, which I might largely insist upon to prove from Scripture.

Now though this be not an idol of the first kind, it is without doubt an idol of the second. It is setting up man's invention instead of God's solemn ordinance, which is a sin for which God plagued the people in Leviticus 10:1–2. It is an image of true baptism set up in the room of it, but not the same, and that in all the before mentioned essentials. A false administrator, ignorant of the true nature of the ordinance instead of a true minister; sprinkling instead of dipping; a carnal infant instead of a true believing man or woman. And all this done at the naming of so many words only, whereas the commission enjoins that they should dip them in the name of the Father, Son, and Holy Ghost. So that there is, in this christening of children, nothing of God's appointment or of what he commanded, namely, the minister wrong, the subject wrong, the form wrong, and also the naming of so many words only instead of dipping into the name of the Father, Son, and Holy Ghost, whereas the commission enjoins the true minister should dip a disciple into the name of Father, Son, and Holy Ghost.

Now let any soul seriously judge whether God can own that which hath nothing of his own appointment or commands, but in every particular contrary thereunto.

But seeing the main thing usually controverted is about the subject, whether infant or believer, I shall leave what I have said, concluding the administration upon children corrupt in all the three foresaid heads, as well as in the last, and shall speak of the last only, namely, that carnal children are not lawful subjects of baptism, and shall begin to speak to the main argument or ground usually pleaded by all, except Papists,[50] for children's baptism, and that is,

Though there be no command nor example, yet there is a consequence, namely, the covenant of life being made to believers and their seed coming out of their loins; baptism, being an ordinance of that covenant, doth also belong to them.

Now I shall endeavour to prove the falseness and erroneousness of this consequence. That it cannot be of God, my first ground, is because it doth oppose itself to the express laws and commands of the New Testament, and whatsoever consequence men do draw from Scripture that crosseth the plain commands of God, to be sure, cannot be of God, but such consequence must needs be, according to Scripture light, of Satan, or at the best from the vision of a man's own heart.

Now this I would have you seriously to take notice of, that baptism of believers is a solemn ordinance of the New Testament enjoined by divers special commands and encouraged with promises of remission of sins and salvation on the right performance of the same.

Now for any man to force a consequence that shall oppose itself against so solemn an ordinance cannot be of God because God cannot speak that which is contrary to himself or to his own commands. As for instance,

---

[50] The Papists do hold that the ordinance of baptism doth convey grace by the very work done, which is so generally confuted by all Protestant authors that I think it not worth my time to speak to that gross error.

When Christ began to teach to his disciples that the Son of Man must suffer many things and be rejected of the elders and chief priests and scribes, and be killed, and the third day rise, he spake that saying openly, and Peter took him and began to rebuke him. But he rebuked Peter, saying, "Get thee behind me Satan."[51] From whence we may observe,

That whatsoever consequence or argument any man shall seem to enforce, though pretending Scripture for the same, that oppose themselves against duty, or do hinder the servants of God therein, I may say of such consequences, and such arguments, "Get thee behind me Satan, thou art an offence unto me." It's clear that Christ concludes those arguments and persuasions, whatsoever they be that do tend to the hinderance of any solemn duty or ordinance of God, of the devil. Get thee behind me, Satan.

Therefore, all those books and arguments set out for the maintenance of children's baptism, grounded upon this consequence, oppose themselves against duty, as you have heard, which is that every penitent or believing person ought to be baptized.

Now the whole tendency of those books being to oppose the practice of the same and to hinder it, I may say of them as Christ said before, etc., for upon this ground we may conclude all those discourses not to be of God. I shall, therefore, leave what is said to you, seriously to weigh whether or no this is not an erroneous consequence.

But in the next place, let us come nearer to examine this consequence, both in itself and the grounds from whence it is drawn.

---

[51] [Matt. 16:23; Mark 8:33.]

2

THE COVENANTS OF LIFE AND
WORKS IN ABRAHAM

he grounds of this consequence is that the covenant of grace belongs to the children of believers. The consequence is, therefore, baptism, being an ordinance of that covenant, must needs belong to the children of believers, in which too lies our whole business. For the grounds of this consequence is brought the covenant of circumcision that belongs to Abraham and his seed after him in their generation.[1]

From hence it is gathered that the covenant of grace, namely, of eternal life, belongs to believers and their seed born of their body. For the covenant God made to Abraham and his offspring, namely, the covenant of circumcision, belonged to Abraham and his seed in their generation. Therefore, circumcision, the sign of the covenant, belonged to them. And so, the new covenant now belongs to believing Gentiles and their seed.

Baptism, being an ordinance of that covenant, belongs also to believing Gentiles and their seed, this being the only and alone foundation ground of all those, except Papists, for their rantizing,

---

[1] Gen. 17:7, 10–14.

or sprinkling of children.

We shall endeavour to prove this ground, from whence this consequence flows, to be so far from being the truth that it is an error, and yea such an error that if it were maintained with all those errors that naturally must needs be defended as consequences of this opinion, it would shake the foundations of the gospel. But that I may, with as much clear satisfaction, inform others, as God had clearly convinced my own soul of the truth of this, I shall propound this method to be handled.

First, I shall make it appear to you that there is two covenants held forth in Scripture, the one a covenant of grace and the other a covenant of works, or an absolute covenant and a conditional covenant.

Secondly, I shall prove that the covenant of circumcision was no covenant of eternal life, but a conditional covenant, a covenant of works.

Thirdly, I shall prove that none but believers ever had, or shall have, right to the covenant of grace.

Fourthly, I shall endeavour to answer such Scriptures, especially those in the New Testament, that are usually alleged for defense of a covenant of life in the flesh.

I. TWO COVENANTS HELD FORTH IN SCRIPTURE

To the first, that there is two covenants mentioned in Scripture is very plain—the one a covenant of eternal life, the other a covenant of works, in which eternal life was not conveyed or given, as appears in Jeremiah 31:31–34.

> Behold, the days come, saith the LORD, that I will make

a new covenant with the house of Israel, and with the house of Judah: Not according to the covenant that I made with their fathers in the day that I took them by the hand to bring them out of the land of Egypt; which my covenant they brake, although I was an husband unto them, saith the Lord: But this shall be the covenant that I will make with the house of Israel; After those days, saith the Lord, I will put my law in their inward parts, and write it in their hearts; and will be their God, and they shall be my people. And they shall teach no more every man his neighbour, and every man his brother, saying, Know the Lord: for they shall all know me, from the least of them unto the greatest of them, saith the Lord: for I will forgive their iniquity, and I will remember their sin no more.

You have here set forth two covenants—the one old, the other new. And as here we find a new and old covenant, so there is likewise mention of two covenants in Hebrews 8, where you have upon the matter the very same words, only it is clear that Jesus Christ is the minister of the new covenant in the 6th and 7th verses of that chapter. "But now hath he obtained a more excellent ministry, by how much also he is the mediator of a better covenant, which was established upon better promises. For if that first covenant had been faultless, then should no place have been sought for the second."

In which place, we may understand two covenants, a new covenant and an old covenant, and Jesus Christ holding himself to be the peculiar minister of the new covenant, unto the church then gathered, all those that are in Christ being God's Israel, Abraham's seed.

"If ye be Christ's, then are ye Abraham's seed, and heirs according to the promise."[2] So that those that are Christ's have this covenant now made to them. And it appears at the 3rd verse that the other covenant was a mere covenant of works in that he saith he hath made the first old.

And now, that which "waxeth old is ready to vanish away,"[3] whereby old covenant he means that typical covenant of works which runs upon the fleshly line of Abraham till Christ came out of the flesh of Abraham, and so put an end to that covenant in the flesh. And this you have further proved in Hebrews 9:15–16. There is again mention made of two covenants or testaments, the first and second. The first was confirmed by the blood of goats and calves, the second by the blood of Christ. Now if any please but to search these Scriptures, it will appear that there is two real distinct covenants or testaments, the one of grace and the other of works—the one conditional, the other absolute.

Now an absolute covenant is a covenant without all condition required in the creature, but what God himself performs, as Jeremiah 32:40, "And I will make an everlasting covenant with them, that I will not turn away from them, to do them good; but I will put my fear in their hearts, that they shall not depart from me," where you see God undertakes both. First, that he will not leave or forsake his people, but do them good. And secondly, undertakes that he will plant his fear in their hearts that they shall not

---

[2] Gal. 3:29.
[3] [Heb. 8:13.]

28

depart from him.

And as in Hebrews 8, he engaged that he will write his law in their hearts, and that he will be their God and they shall be his people, and that he will teach them to know him, and will pardon their iniquities, and their sins he will remember no more.

Now here is nothing but what God hath undertaken to perform and to work in the creature, as further appears in Ezekiel 16:59–60,

> For thus saith the LORD GOD; I will even deal with thee as thou hast done, which hast despised the oath in breaking the covenant. Nevertheless I will remember my covenant with thee in the days of thy youth, and I will establish unto thee an everlasting covenant.

And as he saith afterward, "not by thy covenant,"[4] but by *my* covenant. So that which he calls thy covenant was that which they broke and therein despised the oath, as he saith plainly, holding forth that it was a covenant of works, answerable to that in Nehemiah 10:29, "They clave to their brethren, their nobles, and entered into a curse, and into an oath, to walk in God's law, which was given by Moses the servant of God."

In which case you may discern here was two covenants, the one that God calls his covenant and another, that was their covenant, a covenant of works which they broke. And likewise, you have further the covenant of eternal life opened in Ezekiel 36:25–27,

> Then will I sprinkle clean water upon you, and ye shall be clean: from all your filthiness, and from all your idols,

---

[4] [Eze 16:61.]

will I cleanse you. And a new heart also will I give you, and a new spirit will I put within you: and I will take away the stony heart out of your flesh, and I will give you an heart of flesh. And I will put my spirit within you, and cause you to walk in my statutes, and ye shall keep my judgments, and do them.

Where you have, as I said before, this new covenant wholly lying on God's part, that he would first cleanse them from all their idols and iniquities, that he undertakes to give a new heart, to take away the heart of stone and to give them hearts of flesh, and that he will give the soul his own Spirit, and thereby came these to walk in his ways whom he calls to the obedience of his truth.

If they sin, he binds himself to pardon their sins and to remember their sins and transgressions no more, so that it is impossible that this covenant should be broke, or that a soul shall ever miscarry, that is, once in this covenant, as in respect of his everlasting estate.

And to this purpose, David very eminently speaks in 2ⁿᵈ Samuel 23:5, "Although my house be not so with God; yet he hath made with me an everlasting covenant, ordered in all things, and sure: for this is all my salvation, and all my desire, although he make it not to grow." Where you have David setting out the covenant of grace and the mercies in it to be in all points perfect and sure.

And to this purpose, the prophet in the Isaiah 55:3, inviting souls and persuading them to come to Christ, saith, "Incline your ear, and come unto me: hear, and your soul shall live; and I will make an everlasting covenant with you, even the sure mercies of

David." That is, he will give a soul those new covenant mercies which are, most sure, no way depending upon any condition to be performed in the creature, but wholly upon the Lord, as appears in Psalm 89:28–37,

> My mercy will I keep for him for evermore, and my covenant shall stand fast with him. His seed also will I make to endure for ever, and his throne as the days of heaven. If his children forsake my law, and walk not in my judgments; If they break my statutes, and keep not my commandments; Then will I visit their transgression with the rod, and their iniquity with stripes. Nevertheless my lovingkindness will I not utterly take from him, nor suffer my faithfulness to fail. My covenant will I not break, nor alter the thing that is gone out of my lips. Once have I sworn by my holiness that I will not lie unto David. His seed shall endure for ever, and his throne as the sun before me. It shall be established for ever as the moon, and as a faithful witness in heaven. *Selah*.

Now in these words you have the covenant of eternal life made with Christ and his spiritual seed, which David and his seed were types of, which covenant is a sure covenant to all those to whom it is once made. And to this doth the author to the Hebrews allude when he saith in 6:17–18,

> Wherein God, willing more abundantly to shew unto the heirs of promise the immutability of his counsel, confirmed it by an oath: That by two immutable things, in which it was impossible for God to lie, we might have a strong consolation, who have fled for refuge to lay hold

upon the hope set before us.

Now in this covenant before spoken to, you have both the promise and oath here spoken of, and here in this covenant must needs be discovered the immutability of his counsel, because this is, as David saith, a covenant that is in all points perfect and sure.[5] And James, in his epistle, alluding to these new covenant blessings or gifts, saith, "Every good gift and every perfect gift is from above, and cometh down from the Father of lights, with whom is no variableness, neither shadow of turning."[6] And that he doth here speak of the new covenant gifts doth appear in the next words. He saith, "Of his own will begat he us with the word of truth, that we should be a kind of firstfruits of his creatures."[7]

Now consider well that in this covenant there is nothing that he requires, but he engageth himself to enable us to accomplish. If he command to pray, he promiseth to give his Spirit to help our infirmities; if he command to walk in all his ways, as you have heard, he promiseth that he will put his Spirit in them to cause them to walk in his ways.

OBJECTION

But some may object and say that we find the gospel is held out upon [a] condition of faith and repentance.

ANSWER. It is true. The promise of salvation and remission of sin is held out with a condition to the world because it is God's free mercy to work that condition in the hearts of his elect by

---

[5] [2 Sam. 23:5.]

[6] [Jas. 1:17.]

[7] [Jas. 1:18.]

means of preaching and tendering of the gospel, and in them only.

But we are not to think that this grace of faith and repentance are any qualifications that persons are to attain by their own abilities unto which the gospel is tendered. But in the new covenant, the Lord undertakes to work the condition, and to give the salvation tendered upon that condition also, for saith he, "I will be unto you a God, and you shall be unto me a people."[8] And in particular, he saith he will put his law in their hearts, and in their minds will he write them, and he will teach them to know him.

Now, doubtless, the law of faith and repentance are here included, according to those Scriptures. "For by grace are ye saved through faith; and that not of yourselves: it is the gift of God."[9] Where he holds forth that though faith be an instrumental means of our salvation, yet it is God's free gift wrought in us, and therefore surely a covenant gift. Paul, upon this ground, in Philippians 1:28 saith it is not only given us to believe, but to suffer for his name's sake, where to believe it is given of God. And so, in Acts 18:27, speaking of Apollo, [he] saith that when he came, he helped them much who had believed through grace, as in Hebrews 12:2 where Jesus is said to be as well the author as the finisher of our faith. All which passages do shew that faith is as well given in the new covenant as the salvation tendered upon that condition.

And so, repentance is also a new covenant gift, as well as remission of sins tendered upon that condition, as you find in Acts 5:31, "Him hath God exalted with his right hand to be a Prince

---

[8] [cf. Jer. 11:4.]
[9] Eph 2:8.

and a Saviour, for to give repentance to Israel, and forgiveness of sins." And in Acts 11:18, "When they heard these things, they held their peace, and glorified God, saying, Then hath God also to the Gentiles granted repentance unto life."

Where observe, to God's Israel, both of Jews and Gentiles, God doth grant and freely give repentance, as well as salvation and remission of sins, promised upon the condition of repentance, as likewise appears in 2 Timothy 2:25, where the ministers of God are commanded, in meekness, to instruct those that oppose themselves, if God peradventure will at any time give them repentance to the acknowledging of the truth, which doth plainly prove that though repentance and faith be the condition that the gospel is tendered on, yet you see the Lord doth in the new covenant give faith and repentance as well as remission of sins, and eternal life.

And further, I shall make it appear that this covenant of grace to eternal life was first more obscurely and darkly revealed to our first parents, God directing his speech to the devil in Genesis 3:15. For the greater terror of the devil and the greater comfort of his elect, God saith, "And I will put enmity between thee and the woman, and between thy seed and her seed; it shall bruise thy head, and thou shalt bruise his heel."

This speech contains, in substance, the covenant of grace, Christ, the true spiritual seed, being here promised—who in Scripture is held forth to be the very substance and marrow of the new covenant. Therefore, the Lord saith in Isaiah 42:6, speaking of Christ, "I will give thee for a covenant of the people, for a light of the Gentiles," where the very gift of Christ is called a covenant

34

because where he is promised, all heavenly and spiritual blessings in him are there given, all the promises being in Christ, "Yea, and in him Amen."[10] And all spiritual and heavenly blessings are in him.[11] He saith he will put enmity between the seed of the serpent and the seed of the woman, which must needs have thus much in it.

That God would put, or infuse, in the seed of the woman his created gifts of holiness and purity, and that precious love of God, whereupon it must needs be that this new nature would be hated by the devil as being opposite to him, and also must needs hate the devil with his evil nature, as the psalmist saith, "Ye that love the LORD, hate evil."[12] Christ tells us in Matthew 10:34,

> Think not that I am come to send peace on earth: I came not to send peace, but a sword. For I am come to set a man at variance against his father, and the daughter against her mother, and the daughter in law against her mother in law. And a man's foes shall be they of his own household.

And Luke saith five in one house shall be divided, three against two, and two against three.[13] And what should occasion this division, but that new nature which the Lord infuseth into his own seed or children, which cannot comply with the seed of the serpent? So Peter saith, they spake evil of us, because we run not with them to the same excess of riot.[14]

---

[10] 2 Cor. 1:20.

[11] Eph. 1:3.

[12] [Psa. 97:10.]

[13] Luke 12:52.

[14] 1 Pet. 4:4.

So that I understand that here in Genesis 3 is the whole new covenant included. This new covenant was never entailed upon any fleshly line or generation, as the covenant of circumcision was, but was still confirmed of God in Christ, and to such souls only in Christ, as you find in the promise to Abraham, "In thee shall all the nations of the earth be blessed."[15]

Where you may observe that here is no respect of persons in the matter of these blessings to everlasting life. But all nations, in Christ, as well one nation as another, if in Christ, have those blessings promised to them, and thus much is employed in that promise that all nations out of him are accursed.

But God here directs his speech to Abraham, some may say, it is true, but with respect to Christ now, who as touching the flesh was in his loins, and this blessedness or justification of life which was confirmed in Abraham as a father of all nations is by the apostle Paul called the gospel. "And the scripture, foreseeing that God would justify the heathen through faith, preached before the gospel unto Abraham, saying, In thee shall all nations be blessed." [16] So this blessedness, spoken of in Genesis 12:3, is expounded by Paul to be justification by faith in Christ, and in Acts 3. This blessedness is there expounded to be a turning of every one of them from their iniquities.[17]

And also, this gospel promise or covenant is spoken to in Genesis 15:5, where he bids Abraham look up to the heavens, and if he could number the stars of heaven, and the sands upon the seashore, so shall thy seed be. And Abraham believed God,

---

[15] Gen. 12:3.
[16] Gal. 3:8.
[17] Acts 3:26.

and it was accounted to him for righteousness. This promise is quoted by the apostle Paul as the gospel covenant in Romans 4:3, in opposition to the covenant of circumcision entailed upon the flesh or fleshly line of Abraham. For circumcision was a covenant in the flesh, as the apostle calls it, which he also expounds in the first and second verses to be a covenant of works, but more of that hereafter.

Only that which I would observe at present is that the apostle confirms that gospel promise in Genesis 12:3 and 15:5 to be the new covenant, wherein was given, through faith, the justification of life, excluding in this point the covenant of circumcision, called works.[18] And both these covenants are made with Abraham in Genesis 17. There you find the new covenant made with him to the 6th verse, and from the 7th verse to the 14th, the covenant of circumcision in the flesh. The new covenant is expressed in the 3rd verse, where he saith, "As for me, behold, my covenant is with thee, and thou shalt be a father of many nations. Neither shall thy name any more be called Abram, but thy name shall be Abraham; for a father of many nations have I made thee."[19]

This is, by the apostle Paul in Romans 4:17–18, held out to be the covenant of life, which he doth clearly hold distinct and different from the covenant of circumcision in that place, denying that Abraham or his spiritual seed had their justification in the covenant of circumcision, but bringing in this, that Abraham should be a father of many nations, and so shall thy seed be, as that in which Abraham and his spiritual seed, whether of Jews or

---

[18] Rom. 4:1–2.
[19] [Gen. 17:4–5.]

Gentiles were and should be justified.

And this promise, or covenant, is made with Abraham in Genesis 18:18. In thee shall all the nations of the earth be blessed. So long as Christ was according to the flesh in Abraham's loins, the promise runs thus in thee, meaning that through Christ, which then was in him, should all nations of the earth be blessed.

But as soon as Isaac was come out of Abraham's loins, as in Genesis 22:18, then saith he, "And in thy seed shall all the nations of the earth be blessed." Whereby seed, most strictly, is to be understood Christ, as the apostle Paul intimates in Galatians 3:16, where he expounds this word seed to be not seeds, as of many, but seed as of one, which is Christ. So this blessedness in the seed, Christ is here expounded to be God's confirming his covenant in Christ. And note that this blessedness which David holds out to be the covenant confirmed of God in Christ, it was not entailed upon the flesh of Abraham and his fleshly seed, but made in Abraham as a father of all the spiritual seed in all nations, and confirmed in the seed Christ to all nations.

Here the Jews, after the flesh, have no more interest than any other nation, except it be by faith, for faith only unites to this seed, and gives an inbeing in the same.

This blessedness is expounded by David in Psalm 32:11 to lie in remission of sins, and purgation of the heart from guile, and expounded by the apostle in Acts 3:26 to be a turning everyone from his iniquities, for so there Peter expounds this blessedness, confirmed in Abraham and his seed. And though Christ did fulfill this covenant to the elect of the Jews, yet the rest were hardened, and were never in this sense blest, either in the point of justification or purgation from sin, because they were never in Christ the true seed by faith, nor never were thereby the spiritual seed of Abraham, walking in the steps of his faith, as all his spiritual seed did. "And if ye be Christ's, then are ye Abraham's seed, and heirs according to the promise."[20]

Thus, I have given you from [the] clear light of Scripture that there were two covenants, a covenant of grace and a covenant of works. The covenant of grace belonging to Abraham and his spiritual seed in Christ, and all along from Adam to all the spiritual seed of the woman that were born of promise, as the apostle describes the spiritual seed in Romans 9:8. For he saith, such are accounted the seed that are so born of promise. And so, at this day, all nations, both Jews and Gentiles, that are born again, they are the seed and children that only have an interest in the promise of salvation. And so much for this first head.

II. THE COVENANT OF CIRCUMCISION
AS A COVENANT OF WORKS

Now I come in the next place to prove that the covenant of circumcision is no covenant of eternal life, but a typical covenant, yea a covenant of works, which is also called by the Lord "a covenant in the flesh," and therefore, to be sure, no covenant of eternal life.[21]

But for the better clearing of the truth of this, I shall first expound some words in the covenant, and that is the word "everlasting covenant." That word seems to some to hold it forth a

---

[20] Rom. 4:12 and Gal. 3:29.
[21] Gen. 17:13.

covenant of life because it is said to be everlasting, whereas the word everlasting used in this covenant is to be understood only for the *ever* of the law, for the time of the Jewish state, as always the word is to be understood when applied to the Jews in their generation. As for example, in Leviticus 16 it is said the priest should make an atonement for the holy sanctuary, an atonement for the tabernacle of the congregation, and for the altar, and he shall make an atonement for the priests, and for all the people of the congregation, and this shall be an everlasting statute to you: to make an atonement for the children of Israel for all their sins once a year. Which, everlasting here must needs be understood but till Christ came. And so, in Numbers 25:13, "And he shall have it, and his seed after him, even the covenant of an everlasting priesthood; because he was zealous for his God, and made an atonement for the children of Israel." Speaking here only of a ceremonial priesthood, typing out Jesus Christ, the substance that was to put an end to it.

And so, this covenant of circumcision is to be understood as everlasting as Canaan, and the possession thereof, which was until Christ's coming, who was the substance thereof. This being a maxim, that wheresoever the word "everlasting" or "ever" hath this joined with it, "to you," or "to your seed in their generations," that then it is to be understood only, for the "ever" of the law, and the time and period of that ministration till Christ come, and no longer. "And thou shalt anoint them, as thou didst anoint their father, that they may minister unto me in the priest's office: for their anointing shall surely be an everlasting priesthood through-

40

out their generations."[22] And so, you have it in Exodus 30:20–21, Moses saying,

> When they go into the tabernacle of the congregation, they shall wash with water, that they die not; or when they come near to the altar to minister, to burn offering made by fire unto the LORD: So they shall wash their hands and their feet, that they die not: and it shall be a statute for ever to them, even to him and to his seed throughout their generations.

The next word that I would speak to is, "I will be to thee a God, and to thy seed after thee,"[23] which to some seems to hold forth a covenant of grace, in that he gives himself as a God in this covenant.

To which I answer that God either gives and makes himself over in a covenant of works, which is upon a condition of works done in the creature, or else he gives himself in an absolute covenant of grace in Christ Jesus the mediator, without all condition of works to be fulfilled in the creature.

ARGUMENTS TO PROVE CIRCUMCISION
A COVENANT OF WORKS

ARGUMENT 1. I shall make it clear that God no otherwise gives himself in the covenant of circumcision but conditionally, which is the first argument that I shall use to prove the covenant of circumcision to be a covenant of works and not a covenant of eternal life, because it is conditional. What God promiseth to be

---

[22] Exod. 40:15.
[23] [Gen. 17:7.]

41

or to give to Abraham and his fleshly seed in their generations, it was upon a condition that Abraham and his seed should keep his covenant on their parties, as clearly appears [in] Genesis 17:7–14, where you find the Lord engageth himself to Abraham and his fleshly seed to be their God and to give them the whole land of Canaan. In that sense, he would be their God, to possess them of that good land, and all the blessings of the same, upon condition that they should keep his covenant on their part, both he and his generation after him.

And the subject matter of the covenant that they should keep is that he should be circumcised, and circumcise all born in his house and bought with money. But though circumcision only be here mentioned, yet all the works of the law at that time made known to Abraham are there included, as the apostle expounds it, who best understood that Scripture.[24] For circumcision verily profiteth if thou keep the law. But if thou be a breaker of the law, thy circumcision shall be made uncircumcision, and so you have it. "Stand fast," saith the apostle, "therefore in the liberty wherewith Christ hath made us free, and be not entangled again with the yoke of bondage."[25] Which in Acts 15, it is said neither they, nor their fathers, were able to bear.[26] But Galatians 5:2–3, "Behold, I Paul say unto you, that if ye be circumcised, Christ shall profit you nothing. For I testify again to every man that is circumcised, that he is a debtor to do the whole law."

And so, much is clearly held forth in Galatians 6:12–13, where saith the apostle,

---

[24] Rom. 2:25.
[25] Gal. 5:1–3.
[26] [Acts 15:10.]

As many as desire to make a fair shew in the flesh, they constrain you to be circumcised; only lest they should suffer persecution for the cross of Christ. For neither they themselves who are circumcised keep the law; but desire to have you circumcised, that they may glory in your flesh.

Where you may observe that for men to be circumcised themselves, and not to keep the law, or otherwise to press it upon others, the apostle holds it to be absurd if, withal, they did not keep the law that were thus circumcised.

And in the text before quoted, it is clear that circumcision, in the nature of it, binds them over to keep the law. And to this purpose you find in Acts 15:1, "And certain men which came down from Judaea taught the brethren, *and said*, Except ye be circumcised after the manner of Moses, ye cannot be saved."

Upon which, the apostles come together, and in the 10ᵗʰ verse Peter saith, "Now therefore why tempt ye God, to put a yoke upon the neck of the disciples, which neither our fathers nor we were able to bear?" And what was this yoke, but that they were to be circumcised and to keep the law?

So that circumcision was that which did comprehend under it the covenant of works, or the yoke of bondage that Paul in Galatians 5:1–3 bids Christians stand fast in their liberty, or freedom, from that covenant or yoke of bondage which Jesus Christ had freed them from.

So that you may see that all the observation of the law, which we are set at liberty from by Christ Jesus [in] his death, was included in the law of circumcision. So that in effect, here you have the covenant: Abraham, as if God should say, I will be a God to thee, and to thy seed after thee in their generations, to protect, defend, and deliver thee, to bless thee and thy seed with the blessing of Canaan, to bless thee, and the fruit of thy womb, in the basket, and in their store, in all their outward blessings, upon condition that thou and they will be circumcised and keep the law. Thus, God makes a covenant upon condition, so that if they fail on their part, then he is left at liberty to fail on his part, as that notable expression in Jeremiah 11:2–5,

> Hear ye the words of this covenant, and speak unto the men of Judah, and to the inhabitants of Jerusalem; And say thou unto them, Thus saith the LORD God of Israel; Cursed be the man that obeyeth not the words of this covenant, Which I commanded your fathers in the day that I brought them forth out of the land of Egypt, from the iron furnace, saying, Obey my voice, and do them, according to all which I command you: so shall ye be my people, and I will be your God: That I may perform the oath which I have sworn unto your fathers, to give them a land flowing with milk and honey, as it is this day.

Whence you may clearly observe that God gives himself to be their God and the blessing of Canaan, upon condition that they would keep the law. "So shall ye be my people, and I will be your God."

Now you must mind that Abraham had a new covenant of life made with him when he was seventy-five years old, which was twenty-four years before this time that he had the covenant of circumcision. And his happiness with all his spiritual seed was, and

44

is, in that absolute covenant confirmed of God in Christ, which stands in force still to believers in all nations.[27] But this covenant of circumcision was conditional, and not absolute, therefore no covenant of life, but a covenant of works.

ARGUMENT 2. The second ground why the covenant of circumcision must needs be a covenant of works, a typical covenant, is because it was a national covenant, a covenant in the flesh, as in Genesis 17:13, "He that is born in thy house, and he that is bought with thy money, must needs be circumcised: and my covenant shall be in your flesh for an everlasting covenant." To be sure, such is not the covenant of grace to eternal life, for that was confirmed of God in Christ, as you hear, to all nations. "In thee shall all the nations of the earth be blessed," and "in thy seed shall all the nations of the earth be blessed," as I have formerly spoken to.[28]

But the Lord saith of this covenant of circumcision that it shall be in their flesh for an everlasting covenant. It is manifest by the apostle Paul that this is therefore a covenant of works. Saith he, "What shall we say then that Abraham our father, as pertaining to the flesh, hath found? For if Abraham were justified by works, he hath whereof to glory; but not before God."[29]

These words are inserted by the apostle Paul for the prevention of an objection that might justly be in the mind of the Romans, occasioned by the apostle's former answer. For though the apostle had granted in the beginning of the third chapter that the circumcised Jews were, in some respect, privileged above other

---

[27] Gen. 12:4.
[28] Gen. 12:3; 22:18.
[29] Rom. 4:1–2.

nations, and that chiefly in those eminent tenders and offers that the gospel held out amongst them, which though it proved not effectual to all, yet he minds to some it was effectual. But yet, after in Romans 3:9, the apostle begins to manifest his understanding that to be a Jew after the flesh, and to be in the covenant of circumcision, did not free men from the guilt of damnation no more than other men that were heathens, that were not Jews after the flesh, neither circumcised.

To this purpose, he states a question, "What then? are we better than they? No, in no wise: for we have before proved both Jews and Gentiles, that they are all under sin; As it is written, There is none righteous, no, not one."[30] Where the apostle goes on to prove that the Jews after the flesh, in the covenant of circumcision, were equally in a damnable and sinful condition with the poor heathenish infidels, all equally guilty before God.[31] And his inference is in Romans 3:20 that, therefore, by the works of the law no flesh should be justified in his sight, clearly holding forth that to be a Jew and circumcised and to be under the law is the self-same thing. And when the apostle had concluded that being a Jew in the covenant of circumcision did in no way difference him from the heathen as to life, he now shews what way both Jews and Gentiles come to the justification of life, and that is freely by God's grace through the redemption that is in Christ Jesus, whom God hath set forth to be a propitiation through faith in his blood. And therefore, he excludes the law of works wholly in the matter of justification and brings in the law of faith, shewing clearly that he hath but one way to justify both Jew and Gentile,

[30] [Rom. 3:9–10.]
[31] Rom. 3:19.

which is by faith in Jesus Christ, the true promised seed in the new covenant.

Upon these words the Romans seemed thus to argue.[32] Is it so that a man may be a Jew, and have interest in the covenant of circumcision entailed upon the fleshly line, and seed of Abraham, and yet be not better than pagans or heathens as to the matter of life? What shall we then say that Abraham, our father as appertaining to the flesh, hath found? As if they should say, if a man may be a Jew of the seed of Abraham, and so of the covenant of circumcision, and as to the matter of justification and eternal life be no nearer than a profane Gentile, that is, not Abraham's seed, nor hath any interest in the covenant, what privilege doth Abraham find in the covenant appertaining to, or entailed on the flesh?

Unto which the apostle answers in the 2nd and 3rd verses, and so along in the fourth chapter of the Romans, clearly distinguishing two covenants: the one of circumcision, a covenant of works, the other a promise of Jesus Christ made to the faith of such as believe. Therefore, saith the apostle in the 2nd verse and so forward, "If Abraham were justified by works, he hath wherof to glory, but not before God," plainly interpreting that the covenant that our father Abraham had interest in, as appertaining to the flesh of him and his seed after him in their generations, was a covenant of works in which Abraham had nothing to glory in before God. The reason is given because he was justified before God in another covenant or promise.[33] For what saith the Scripture? "Abraham believed God, and it was counted unto him for

---

[32] Rom. 4:1.

[33] Gen. 15:5–6.

righteousness."[34]

And thus, the apostle goes along shewing that justification was not to be had in the covenant of works entailed on the flesh of Abraham, but by faith in the covenant of grace, the promised seed, which he proves by David's testimony in Psalm 32:1–2, set down in verses 6–8 of this chapter.

Now thus much being said, he states the question whether this grace of justification came upon the circumcision only, or the uncircumcision also, for we say that faith was reckoned unto Abraham for righteousness.

Now here is the question, seeing that Abraham had two covenants made with him—one the gospel of faith, and the other a covenant in the flesh—in which of these had he his justification to eternal life?

The answer is plain, for saith the apostle, not in circumcision. He was not justified in or by the covenant of circumcision, but in the promise of the promised seed, which God is said to give a covenant for his people by faith in that seed. Even in uncircumcision was Abraham justified, and that, as I said before, twenty-four years before the covenant of circumcision was made with him. He was justified believing in the promise of the Messiah that was to come out of his loins, according to the flesh, "In whom all nations of the earth should be blessed."[35]

Now God promised that the Messiah according to the flesh should come out of Abraham, namely, out of his loins or his flesh, and this was then a great article of his faith that he was to believe to righteousness, not only that justification was to be had, and

[34] [Rom. 4:3.]
[35] [Gen. 12:3.]

blessedness to be had, but it must be had in that seed that was to come out of Abraham according to the flesh.

And as a confirmation and seal of this public righteousness, confirmed in Abraham as a father of all nations, God elects that flesh and blood to himself; I mean the family of Abraham in an external covenant, to point out to all the world, that as verily as God did take this nation, according to the flesh, to himself by this external covenant, so would God be incarnate in this flesh.

And as the flesh of the foreskin of the member of generation must be cut or bruised, and the bloodshed by which the Jew, according to the flesh, was bound to keep the law, this, I understand, did figure out how Christ, the true seed of Abraham, descending out of his loins by generation, should, considered as male and not female, by breaking his flesh and shedding his blood, fulfil and satisfy the law.

So that this covenant of circumcision was of sealing use to Abraham, to confirm this other covenant, and a schoolmaster to lead to Christ, as all other branches of that old covenant were. Therefore, saith Paul in Romans 4:11, "Moreover he received the sign of circumcision, a seal of the righteousness of the faith which he had yet being uncircumcised: that he might be the father of all them that believe."

Where observe, the apostle calls not circumcision a seal, but a sign. "He received the sign of circumcision, a seal of the righteousness of the faith which he had yet being uncircumcised."[36] There are these reasons in the text that restrain the sealing use of circumcision only to Abraham.

---

[36] [Rom. 4:11.]

First, because this righteousness of faith, the text saith, he had before he was circumcised. Therefore, good reason it might be sealed or confirmed, having it before he received the sign of circumcision, a seal of the righteousness of faith which he had being uncircumcised. But his posterity after him, at eight days old, cannot be said that they had this righteousness of faith to seal, having it not preceding their circumcision.

The second reason the text affords us is that he might be the father of all that believe; this is the main reason the apostle insists upon, "He received the sign of circumcision, a seal of the righteousness of faith…that he might be the father of all them that believe."

This reason cannot be applicable to any of Abraham's posterity besides himself, for they were not the fathers of all that believe; that was proper to Abraham to be a high father, or a father of all nations. Therefore, as I said before, God promised in Abraham that public righteousness, as a father of all nations in the covenant of grace, adds to that covenant an external covenant to be entailed in his line and in his flesh as a confirmation of the same.

A third reason is this: here is the Spirit of God affirming the sealing use of circumcision to Abraham only, and not to any one of his fleshly seed, and, as before, upon a reason special to Abraham. Now where the Scripture hath not a mouth to speak, we must not have an ear to hear. But the Scripture here only affirms circumcision to be a seal of the righteousness of faith to Abraham, and affords no such thing as to his seed.

A fourth reason lies in Romans 4:13, that the promise of Abraham to be the heir of the world was not to him, nor his seed through the law, that is, through the covenant of circumcision, but through the righteousness of faith.

For if they, which are of the law, be heirs, then faith is made void and the promise of none effect, because the law worketh wrath. Therefore, it is of faith that it might be by grace to the end the promises might be sure to all the seed. Not to that only which is of the law, but to that also which is of the faith of Abraham, who is the father of us all. "(As it is written, I have made thee a father of many nations,) before him whom he believed, even God, who quickeneth the dead."[37]

So that there is not in all the Scripture a place [that] more clearly proves the covenant of circumcision entailed on the fleshly line of Abraham to be a covenant of works than this fourth [chapter] of the Romans, clearing and setting the covenant of circumcision and faith in opposition, holding forth that Abraham and all his spiritual seed had their justification in another covenant, and not in the covenant of circumcision, clearly holding forth the covenant of circumcision to be works and not grace, which doth sufficiently prove that the covenant of circumcision had no promise of justification or eternal life in it.

But further, that the covenant entailed on the flesh must needs be understood to be a covenant of works, namely, that of circumcision, appears in Philippians 3:2–4 and so forward, where saith the apostle, "Beware of dogs, beware of evil workers, beware of the concision. For we are the circumcision, which worship God in the spirit, and rejoice in Christ Jesus, and have no confidence in the flesh." By flesh he means the covenant entailed upon the

---

[37] [Rom. 4:17.]

flesh, the covenant of circumcision. It is plain by his answer, for he saith,

> If any other man thinketh that he hath whereof he might trust in the flesh, I more: Circumcised the eighth day, of the stock of Israel, of the tribe of Benjamin, an Hebrew of the Hebrews; as touching the law, a Pharisee; Concerning zeal, persecuting the church; touching the righteousness which is in the law, blameless.[38]

And this he sets by no more than dung or dross in comparison of the other covenant or promise of Christ, righteousness and salvation by him, which he received by faith. And he suffered the loss of all things for the sake of him, and did account all the whole privilege of circumcision, and the covenant of works, to be but as dung that he might win Christ, which if the promise of Christ and salvation and justification by him had been given in the covenant of the flesh, and line of Abraham, then it had been very improper for Paul to account this as dung, and to cast contempt upon it as that which was wholly void of Christ. It would be very sinful for any man, in such a case, to cast such contempt upon the covenant of grace itself and the privileges thereof peculiarly relating to the same.

But you see, Paul doth here clearly distinguish two covenants. The one of faith, the other of circumcision. This will further appear in, "Are ye so foolish? having begun in the Spirit, are ye now made perfect by the flesh?"[39]

Where he again distinguisheth two covenants, the one spiritual, the other a fleshly covenant. The Galatians, having at the

---

[38] [Phil. 3:4–6.]
[39] Gal. 3:3.

52

first hearing of him, begun to embrace the gospel, or the Spirit, or spiritual word of the new covenant, and now they would join the covenant of works in the flesh with the gospel, which it is evident he means the covenant of circumcision, which here they would seek to be perfected by.

Therefore, in Galatians 4 the latter end, he clearly distinguisheth between two covenants under the figure of Sarah and Hagar and two seeds, holding forth the covenant of circumcision to be the covenant of works, and to be that bondwoman, as it were, in chapters 5:1–3 and 6:12–13. So that if you will seriously mind these Scriptures, they do most evidently prove that the covenant of circumcision made in the flesh or fleshly line of Abraham is a covenant of works, and that which the gospel or covenant of grace is set in opposition to, and as this covenant of circumcision is set in opposition to the covenant of eternal life, as having all the works of the law included in it.

So consider the new covenant speaks thus, "I will put my law in your hearts, and in your minds will I write them."[40] But circumcision is a covenant not in the heart, but in the flesh, only as you have heard. This is the second ground why the covenant of circumcision cannot be a covenant of eternal life, but a covenant of works only.

ARGUMENT 3. The third reason to prove circumcision to be a covenant of works and not of eternal life is because there is no promise of eternal life in it, but of temporal blessings in the land of Canaan, and that God promising himself to be a God is only in that respect as to outward protection and provision in the land

---

[40] [Jer. 31:33.]

of Canaan, and other like privileges. And that is noted by the apostle in Hebrews 8:6, "But now hath he obtained a more excellent ministry, by how much also he is the mediator of a better covenant, which was established upon better promises."

Herein he clearly doth shew that the covenant, waxing old and vanishing away, was grounded upon worse promises, which must needs be understood temporal promises, as in Jeremiah 11:2–5,

> Hear ye the words of this covenant, and speak unto the men of Judah, and to the inhabitants of Jerusalem; And say thou unto them, Thus saith the LORD God of Israel; Cursed be the man that obeyeth not the words of this covenant, Which I commanded your fathers in the day that I brought them forth out of the land of Egypt, from the iron furnace, saying, Obey my voice, and do them, according to all which I command you: so shall ye be my people, and I will be your God: That I may perform the oath which I have sworn unto your fathers, to give them a land flowing with milk and honey, as it is this day. Then answered I, and said, So be it, O LORD.

Where you have this covenant of God being his people's God, and giving them Canaan, annexed to the works of the law as being all one covenant.

Observe the words in the text, "So shall ye be my people, and I will be your God: That I may perform the oath which I have sworn unto your fathers, to give them a land flowing with milk and honey." You shall see that the promises of Canaan and the blessings thereof are annexed to the law of works.

> See, I have set before thee this day life and good, and

> death and evil; In that I command thee this day to love
> the LORD thy God, to walk in his ways, and to keep his
> commandments and his statutes and his judgments, that
> thou mayest live and multiply: and the LORD thy God
> shall bless thee in the land whither thou goest to possess
> it.[41]

And so, in the last verse, where he presseth the people to obey
his voice that they might dwell in the land that the Lord sware
unto their fathers, to Abraham, Isaac, and Jacob to give them.
And so, in Deuteronomy 7:12–13,

> Wherefore it shall come to pass, if ye hearken to these
> judgments, and keep, and do them, that the LORD thy
> God shall keep unto thee the covenant and the mercy
> which he sware unto thy fathers: And he will love thee,
> and bless thee, and multiply thee: he will also bless the
> fruit of thy womb, and the fruit of thy land, thy corn, and
> thy wine, and thine oil, the increase of thy kine, and the
> flocks of thy sheep, in the land which he sware unto thy
> fathers to give thee.

So that you see the covenant of God, giving himself a God to
the national people of the Jews in relation to the blessing of Canaan, was still upon obedience to the works of the law. That this
covenant which God elected to himself the body of Israel, in and
by which he separated them to himself from all the nations of the
earth, it is clear was a covenant of works wherein the people were
bound to outward observance and worship and service to God.
Upon this condition would God be their God and give them Ca-

---

[41] Deut. 30:15–16.

naan. For there is a vast difference in Gods making over himself to be a God to a people in a conditional covenant of works out of Christ, and in an absolute covenant established of God in Christ. For in such a covenant, he was never the God of the whole family of Abraham, or church of Israel. The elect obtained that; the rest were hardened, as in Romans 11:17.

ARGUMENT 4. The fourth ground is this: that a man, by laying out a little money, might have brought a person into this covenant and interested him thereby into all the privileges of the same, which if this were a covenant of life wherein the Spirit and spiritual gifts of the Lord had been given, a man might say as Peter did say to Simon Magus, "Thy money perish with thee."[42]

But for that reason, most certain it is that this covenant of circumcision is no spiritual covenant, which will appear from the words of the covenant in Genesis 17:12–13,

> And he that is eight days old shall be circumcised among you, every man child in your generations, he that is born in the house, or bought with money of any stranger, which is not of thy seed. He that is born in thy house, and he that is bought with thy money, must needs be circumcised: and my covenant shall be in your flesh for an everlasting covenant.

Where observe that all bought with money must be circumcised. So that if an Israelite should buy a black moor, or the most savage heathen in the world, he was bound to see him circumcised. And being circumcised, he was now in that covenant. The truth is circumcision was one of those carnal ordinances that the

---

[42] [Acts 8:20.]

author to the Hebrews, in Hebrews 9:9, doth speak of that was appointed till the time of reformation.

Now the person which the Lord would have circumcised must be of the family of Abraham, and that is all the qualifications required. For God doth not require a person so and so spiritually qualified as he doth now under the gospel. The Lord gives, in general, a law and commandment unto Abraham that all his family must be circumcised, and that he must see it performed.

It is not in the institution enjoined that the person that doth circumcise must be a believer, neither is it enjoined that the person upon whom it is done must have discipleship, or the work of grace, but this only: he must be one of the family of Abraham, either born in his house or bought with his money, and so the slave bought with money was as truly interested into the covenant of God, and the right of eating the Passover, as one born in the house of the seed of Abraham.

ARGUMENT 5. A fifth ground is this: that men, out of this covenant, might be saved, and such as were really interested in it might be damned.

As for example, Lot, dwelling in the city of Sodom, and all the godly that day in the whole world, excepting Abraham and his house or family, were no way interested in the covenant of circumcision, yet were saved. And Israel, who, for the multitude of them, were as the sand on the seashore and interested in this covenant, yet but a remnant of them were saved, as Isaiah 10:23. Lot is commended to be a just and righteous man, and yet this covenant was never made to him, nor his seed and posterity, the Ammonites and Moabites, which were as truly the seed and children of a believer as the seed of Abraham were.

So you find Job in the Land of Uz in the Book of Job, and his four friends. And besides those of Job's friends, one of his friends doth intimate several other ancient and godly persons in those times.[43] For saith he, "Ask the ancients and they will tell thee, for we have those with us, much more elder than thy father," which doth argue that there were very ancient godly men fit to be inquired of, as touching those heavenly mysteries, that were much older than Job's father in that east country. And it is plain that neither they, nor any of their children or families, had right to circumcision and the blessing of Canaan. But most sure it is they had interest in the covenant of life, which plainly shews that circumcision was but an earthly typical covenant, such as good and godly men might, nor have interest in, and such as wicked men had an interest in.

Do not we find that all David's sons were in this covenant? But how many, except Solomon, had any right to the covenant of life? Yea, Abraham himself had eight sons, and each of them a generation, but there was none of the other had the covenant of circumcision made with them, but only Isaac, though the rest were as truly the sons of believing Abraham as Isaac was. For Ishmael and the six sons that he had by Keturah with their generations were all the children of the same believing Abraham as Isaac was, and yet this covenant ran not upon either of their posterity. "But, in Isaac," saith the text, "shall thy seed be called," though we may not be so uncharitable but to think that many of the seed of those that went into the east country might be the elect of God and in

---

[43] Job 8:8, 10; 15:10.

THE COVENANTS OF LIFE AND WORKS IN ABRAHAM

a covenant of grace.[44] Yet, be sure, they had not an interest in this covenant of circumcision and the inheritance of Canaan.

And Isaiah tells us in Isaiah 1:9 that if God had not left him a very small remnant, Israel had been as Sodom and Gomorah. So that there was in the whole nation of Israel, that were in the covenant of circumcision, but a very small remnant selected out from the rest into the covenant of life.[45] The apostle so makes use of the words, and in the Romans 11:5, 7. The apostle saith the election in and amongst Israel have obtained it, and the rest were hardened or blinded.

The rest? may some say. What rest? The rest of Israel in the covenant of circumcision. But it is plain that all Israel were elected, one as much as another in the covenant of circumcision, by which they were, as I have said, separated to God from all other nations.

But it is plain that there was a gospel testament confirmed of God in Christ held out and tendered to the Jews by the holy prophets and penmen of God. The elect obtained that and the rest were hardened, remaining still in the literal and old covenant of circumcision which they had only right to by generation.

But this, none could have right to, but by the regeneration and new birth. And therefore, saith Isaiah 8:18, "I and the children whom the LORD hath given me are for signs and for wonders in Israel," implying clearly that a little handful of Israel are given to Christ in the covenant of grace out from amongst the body of Israel. The rest of the multitude of Israel remained without being given to Christ, making signs and wonders at such as were given

---

[44] [Rom. 9:7].
[45] Rom. 9.

to him by being admitted into a covenant of eternal life through faith, which it appears the whole body of Israel were not admitted into, but some few only. So that you see souls may be in this covenant of circumcision and be damned, and out of it and saved. Therefore, this cannot be a covenant of eternal life, but only a typical covenant of works.

ARGUMENT 6. The sixth ground to prove that the covenant of circumcision was but a covenant of works, an outward typical covenant, was this: that this covenant of circumcision might be broken, as the Lord saith in Genesis 17:14. "And the uncircumcised man child whose flesh of his foreskin is not circumcised, that soul shall be cut off from his people; he hath broken my covenant."

Where observe, though he were born of the family, and of the seed of Abraham, and so had an interest in the covenant, yet he might forfeit his right and break this covenant, so as to be cast off from God's people.

This is therefore that old covenant spoke of by Jeremiah 31:31. "I will make a new covenant with the house of Israel, not like that covenant which I made with their fathers, which they broke, and my soul had no pleasure in them." For as I have shewed before, it is impossible that the new covenant can be broken because it is an absolute covenant made on no condition to be fulfilled by the creature, but the Lord works both to will and to do of his good pleasure in this covenant. Therefore, "it is not of him that willeth, nor of him that runneth, but of God that sheweth mercy."[46] Therefore, the Lord, speaking of the new covenant in Jeremiah

---

[46] [Rom. 9:16.]

33:15–21, saith,

> In those days, and at that time, will I cause the Branch of righteousness to grow up unto David; and he shall execute judgment and righteousness in the land. In those days shall Judah be saved, and Jerusalem shall dwell safely: and this is the name wherewith she shall be called, The LORD our righteousness. For thus saith the LORD; David shall never want a man to sit upon the throne of the house of Israel; Neither shall the priests the Levites want a man before me to offer burnt offerings, and to kindle meat offerings, and to do sacrifice continually. And the word of the LORD came unto Jeremiah, saying, Thus saith the LORD; If ye can break my covenant of the day, and my covenant of the night, and that there should not be day and night in their season; Then may also my covenant be broken with David my servant, that he should not have a son to reign upon his throne.

Where you see the spiritual covenant cannot be broken, as Psalm 89:34, "My covenant will I not break, nor alter the thing that is gone out of my lips."

Therefore, it must needs be a covenant of works that is conditional. He made such a covenant with the priest mentioned in 1 Samuel 2:30, where the Lord saith to this purpose,

> Wherefore the LORD God of Israel saith, I said indeed that thy house, and the house of thy father, should walk before me forever: but now the LORD saith, Be it far from me; for them that honour me I will honour, and they that despise me shall be lightly esteemed.

You must still mind those promises the Lord makes upon condition, the creature not walking in the performance of the condition on his part, God is set free or at liberty whether he will perform such conditional promises, yea or no.

But it is not so in absolute promises confirmed of God in Christ.[47] Those promises are all yea and amen, as you see in 2 Corinthians 1:20. But the covenant of circumcision, being a covenant of works, a poor creature truly interested in that covenant might break it, forfeit his interest, and be cast out and rejected out of that covenant from amongst his people, as is clearly confirmed in Isaiah 50:1,

> Thus saith the LORD, Where is the bill of your mother's divorcement, whom I have put away? or which of my creditors is it to whom I have sold you? Behold, for your iniquities have ye sold yourselves, and for your transgressions is your mother put away.

Now, beloved, a divorce argues a breach and forfeiting the covenant, which the body of all Israel was in, and we know all along the national covenant was that of circumcision. And they that know, in the least measure, the nature of the covenant of grace cannot but know it to be such a covenant, out of which a soul cannot be divorced from the Lord.

OBJECTION

But some may say there are many that are visibly in a covenant of grace now under the gospel, and yet may be cast out from God's people. Yet, it followeth not but that it is a covenant of grace. And

---

[47] Gal. 3:17.

so, then, they might be visibly in a covenant of grace and yet be rejected.

ANSWER. Persons may now profess to be in Christ, and so in a covenant of grace by an outward profession, but this being barely a profession and not in truth in them that profess the same. They profess they were in that which in truth they never were. For under the gospel, we have no infallible rule to know who is in the covenant of grace and who not, because we have only the confession of themselves who may deceive themselves and us.

But we have an infallible rule to judge, that Abraham, Isaac, and Jacob, and the seed forward in their loins, or their generations, were in this covenant of circumcision. And therefore, it is a great mistake for any to evade what hath been said upon such a groundless objection.

Now consider that it is that great and faithful God that saith and professeth Abraham [and] his seed and family after him, from Jacob forward, were in this covenant with him. But now it is only poor, unfaithful man, hypocritical, dissembling, [and] proud man that saith he is in the covenant of life when it proves not so, or when it visibly proves the contrary. For saints have a rule to disown such. But this is a most certain truth, that God did never put a soul away and make a divorce between himself and any one soul in a covenant of life. And it is as certain that the whole church of Israel were in reality and truth in the covenant of circumcision, as appears in Genesis 17:10–11, where Abraham and those born in his house are to be circumcised. And so, Psalm 105:9–11, "Which covenant he made with Abraham, and his oath unto Isaac; And confirmed the same unto Jacob for a law, and to Israel for an everlasting covenant: Saying, Unto thee will I give the land of Canaan, the lot of your inheritance."

Now it would plentifully appear, if further proof needed, that God, his own self, testifyeth making and entering into covenant with Abraham, Isaac, and Jacob, and their seed forward. There-fore, let no man please himself with such a poor, groundless ob-jection that the family of Israel were only visibly, or in the judge-ment of charity, in the covenant of circumcision as hypocrites are now in the covenant of grace.

For there is nothing more clear than this: that Israel were in truth and reality in the covenant of circumcision, expressed by the mouth of God himself, and nothing more certain that Israel was never, all of them, so much visibly in the covenant of grace.

For if it were necessary, I could multiply places of Scripture to prove the most part of Israel visibly unbelievers, living in those manifest fruits of the flesh, as drunkenness, swearing, lying, whoring, stealing, covetousness, and palpable ignorance, with-out faith and knowledge, shedding of blood. All these notorious sins were constantly in the greatest part of the church of Israel, that they neighed, as fed horses, after their neighbour's wives, and were given to oppression and horrid idolatry. All these sins being such manifest fruits of the flesh that such as live in them, the apostle saith, cannot enter into the kingdom of Christ and of God, but are visibly the children of the devil. Therefore, to say the whole body of Israel were visibly godly, and so visibly in the covenant of grace, that is a most gross mistake. They were really in the outward national covenant of circumcision, but not the generality so much as visibly in the gospel covenant of life.

For it could not be denied, but that those Jews in John 8:30 and so forward were Abraham's children, and interested in the covenant of works. Yet, Christ is far from concluding their right to the covenant of sonship, the heavenly adoption, but rather in that respect concludeth they are of their father, the devil, whose works they did, they being liars as he was from the beginning, and enemies to Christ, as the devil was. Therefore, he excludes them from being the children of God, so that the main mass of blindness and darkness lying upon men's minds is this: they mix and confound the two covenants made to Abraham—the one a spiritual heavenly covenant made to him as a father of the faithful, and to those only who walk in the steps of faithful Abraham, and the temporal covenant of circumcision to the seed according to the flesh, from Jacob forward, and those joining themselves to that family.

So then, in a word, the covenant of circumcision must needs be a covenant of works, and not of eternal life, because it might be broken, which the covenant of eternal life cannot be.

ARGUMENT 7. The seventh ground to prove the covenant of circumcision not to be a covenant of grace is that if we maintain the covenant of circumcision to be a covenant of grace to eternal life, therein we overthrow many fundamental points of religion, which is a strong ground to prove it is not of grace, but an outward typical covenant. For it is impossible that such understanding of Scripture, which crosseth plain fundamental points of religion, can be true.

Now to give you some example for this, first you must needs

confess that the covenant of circumcision was made to Abraham and his seed after him, in their generations, from Isaac and Jacob forward,[48] so that being born in the house or family of Israel, or being bought with the money of one of the Israelites, interested a person in that covenant, he coming forth of that line was born heir to that covenant and the privileges of the same.

Now consider that the chief and precious privileges of the covenant of grace are adoption or sonship, justification, and the inward work of sanctification, all which privileges that generation must needs be born heirs to if they were born heirs of a covenant of grace, which if this should be asserted, as it is by those who defend children's baptism,[49] then this fundamental point of religion must needs be denied, that all mankind are by nature the children of wrath, and that all both Jews and Gentiles are charged under sin.[50] And there is none righteous, no not one.[51] But be it known to you, this is a fundamental doctrine of truth, generally acknowledged by all the godly, that we are dead in sins and trespasses, wherein in times past we walked according to the course of this world, according to the prince of the power of the air, the spirit that now worketh in the children of disobedience, among whom also we had our conversation in times past, in the lust of the flesh, and of the mind, and were children of wrath by nature as well as others.

Now the apostle Paul affirmeth this to be equally the state of himself, who was born in the church of Israel, as well as the

---

[48] Gen. 17:7.

[49] To say that the covenant of grace is entailed on the flesh overthroweth the main fundamental points of our religion.

[50] Eph. 2:2.

[51] Rom. 3:9.

Gentiles. And David doth affirm this of all in general, which the apostle Paul urgeth in Romans 3:9 forwards, speaking of himself and the rest of the national churches of the Jews.[52] "What then?" saith he, "are we better than they?" meaning than the Gentiles.

> No, in no wise: for we have before proved both Jews and Gentiles, that they are all under sin; As it is written, There is none righteous, no, not one: There is none that understandeth, there is none that seeketh after God. They are all gone out of the way, they are together become unprofitable; there is none that doeth good, no, not one.[53]

And in Psalm 51, David saith, "I was shapen in iniquity; and in sin did my mother conceive me,"[54] who was a child of the church of God, as it is usually termed.

But beloved, this doctrine is clear in Scripture, and clearly experienced by every godly Christian, which truth must needs be overthrown if the whole body of Israel were born adopted sons and heirs of a covenant of eternal life, born heirs of justification; then they were never heirs of wrath, nor in a state of damnation, nor never proved nor charged under sin nor never all unrighteous, because born heirs of a covenant of grace, and of righteousness, nor never born dead in sins and trespasses, for that is inconsistent with being in a covenant of grace and life.

This opinion of holding the covenant of grace to be entailed in the flesh, opposing itself so directly against this forementioned foundation of religion, must needs be a gross error so considered.

The second fundamental point of religion that this error op-

---

[52] Psa. 14:2–3.
[53] Rom. 3:9–12.
[54] [Psa. 51:5.]

poseth itself against is stability in a covenant of eternal life. It cannot be imagined that I should much insist upon proving this doctrine of stability in grace to be a fundamental truth. I shall take that for granted from the nature of the new covenant in several Scriptures before recited, as in Psalm 125, "They that trust in the LORD shall be as mount Zion, which cannot be removed, but abideth for ever. As the mountains are round about Jerusalem, so the LORD is round about his people from henceforth even for ever."[55] And in Psalm 89:33–34, "Nevertheless my lovingkindness will I not utterly take from him, nor suffer my faithfulness to fail. My covenant will I not break, nor alter the thing that is gone out of my lips."

But taking this for granted to be a truth, that all born in the church of the Jews were born heirs of his stable covenant, and so were really and in truth in the covenant of grace, then most of the church of Israel that were in a covenant of grace were damned and not saved, as Isaiah 10:22–23. Though Israel were as the sand of the sea, yet a remnant of them were saved only. And so, Isaiah with Romans 9:27–28, 31, "But Israel, which followed after the law of righteousness, hath not attained to the law of righteousness." Paul saith, Romans 11:5, "There is a remnant according to the election of grace." And in verse 7, how they obtained it, but the rest were hardened; all but the remnant were blinded and hardened.

Therefore, if such multitudes as the sand of the sea were all really in a covenant of grace, most of them must be understood to fall out of the covenant, and so to fall out of the covenant of life.

---

[55] Psa. 125:1–2.

This is another fundamental truth that this opinion is fully against, defending that souls may be truly in a covenant of eternal life, and yet perish and be damned.

The third foundation that this error overthrows is the necessity of conversion or regeneration, which doctrine is eminently confirmed by Christ in the gospel as a fundamental truth, where Christ, speaking to Nicodemus, tells him that except a man be born again of water and of the Spirit, he cannot enter into the kingdom of God.[56] And likewise, in John 8:24, "If ye believe not that I am he, ye shall die in your sins." And John 3:36, "He that believeth not the Son shall not see life."

The before mentioned errors that holds a covenant of life running in the flesh upon the carnal seed opposeth itself against this, for might the carnal seed of Israel say to Christ, why do you preach such a doctrine to us, "that except you be born again, you cannot enter into the kingdom of heaven"? We affirm the contrary, seeing by the first birth we have an interest in the covenant of grace and eternal life already, without believing and being born again, and so are entered into the kingdom of God, and the privileges thereof, whereas you say that except you believe that I am he, you shall die in your sins. Why doth Christ pronounce death without believing, seeing we are acquainted with another way to enter into life than the way of believing, which is to be begotten of one of the church or a believer?

We find the Holy Ghost in 1 John 5:12 saith, "He that hath the Son hath life; and he that hath not the Son of God hath not life." No, saith this error, there were thousands that were interested

---

[56] John 3:4–5.

in life without having Christ, that is to say by carnal generation. Saith the apostle, "There is none other name under heaven given among men, whereby we must be saved."[57] Yea, saith this error, there is another name by which we may come into a covenant of eternal life, and so to be saved, so that here lies the case. Where Christ in the gospel powerfully affirms no other way to life but by believing, regeneration, and coming to Jesus Christ, this opinion destroys all these testimonies, opening another door of entrance into the covenant of life besides this, and that by fleshly generation, though Christ saith to Nicodemus, "That which is born of the flesh is flesh; and that which is born of the Spirit is spirit,"[58] as if souls were infatuated, and had no ears to hear his plain word.

They, of this opinion, do defend the contrary. To what purpose should any man seek the conversion of any of believer's children, whether formerly of the nation of the Jews, or now the nations of the believing Gentiles, seeing they are born heirs of a covenant of eternal life, and so are in as good a state without conversion and believing and being born again as any other soul by believing, and by new birth can be brought into?

This doctrine tends to justify the rebellious Jews against John the Baptist, and against Christ. The Sadducees and Pharisees came to John's baptism. Saith John, "O generation of vipers, who hath warned you to flee from the wrath to come? Bring forth therefore fruits meet for repentance: And think not to say within yourselves, We have Abraham to our father."[59] John, you see, would have this people to be converted to entitle them to this

---

[57] [Acts 4:12.]

[58] John 3:6.

[59] Matt. 3:7–9.

covenant of grace, and so to baptism, which is an ordinance of the same covenant, and not so much as think so erroneously, as if being children to Abraham according to the flesh should entitle them to the same. Therefore, saith he, think not within yourselves we have Abraham as our father, and we are his children according to the flesh, and therefore we need not a work of conversion, or true repentance, to entitle us to the privileges of the covenant, such as was baptism. And also, in John 8:31 and forwards, saith Christ unto some Jews, unto whom he spake,

> If ye continue in my word, then are ye my disciples indeed; And ye shall know the truth, and the truth shall make you free. They answered him, We be Abraham's seed, and were never in bondage to any man: how sayest thou, Ye shall be made free?[60]

Where you may observe these wicked obstinate Jews were of the same opinion, that they were in a state of happiness, good enough by generation by being Abraham's seed, according to the flesh. Jesus answereth, "Whosoever committeth sin is the servant of sin. And the servant abideth not in the house for ever."[61] We find Christ, afterwards, tells these sons of Abraham that they were so far from being the adopted sons of God, in a covenant of life, that they were of their father, the devil. And these same persons Christ speaks to in verse 24, telling them, except they believed Christ was he, they should die in their sins.

Christ was far from this opinion as to think that covenant of circumcision to be a covenant of life, but he doth thoroughly reprehend them for this groundless confidence, which error was the

---

[60] John 8:31–33.
[61] John 8:34–35.

main obstacle that hindered the Jews from faith and repentance, because they thought it entitled them to happiness, enough to be of the stock of Abraham, and to be born heirs of the covenant of circumcision. This very rotten opinion was, to them, one of the devil's sleights to lull them asleep in a carnal and unconverted condition. They thought that needed not, which thought of theirs had been true enough, provided all the children of Abraham had, by generation, interest in the covenant of life, which other men could have no interest in without regeneration. But Christ, you see, presseth a necessity of conversion to these children of Abraham, that at the present were as fully interested in the covenant of circumcision as Abraham himself, even to Nicodemus, who was a ruler of the Jews, Christ presseth a necessity thereof to him, and also labours by a parable in Luke 16 to convince those sottish Jews that one might be the seed of Abraham according to the flesh, and yet be irrecoverably damned. And therefore, he brings in the rich man in hell, speaking thus, "Father Abraham, have mercy on me, and send Lazarus, that he may dip the tip of his finger in water, and cool my tongue."[62] And Abraham is brought in, owning him to be his son, speaking thus, "Son, remember that thou in thy lifetime receivedst thy good things."[63]

Where you may observe that the man in hell, irrecoverably damned, owns Abraham to be his father, and Abraham also doth acknowledge him to be his son. "Son," saith Abraham, where you clearly see man may be a son of Abraham, and yet damned. Thou hadst thy good things in this life, but Lazarus his evil things. Ezekiel 18:9–10, where a just man is presupposed to beget a son that

[62] [Luke 16:24.]
[63] [Luke 16:25.]

is a robber, and a shedder of blood, and that goes out in all manner of wickedness, and that in Israel.

Wherein observe, Abraham owns no other privilege belonged to the rich man by virtue of being the son of Abraham but what was in this life, or in this world. Hell was his best portion in the world to come, which if he had been born heir to the covenant of life, how then could Abraham's affirmation have been true?

Beloved, let all ingenuous spirits that are not willing to walk blindfold consider how contrary to the whole tenor of the gospel this opinion is, and how destructive to this fundamental principle of the gospel the necessity of Christ, of regeneration, and destroys all sense of the necessity of conversion, and helps to harden men to destruction, as it did the blind Jews, who, as it appears, were fully blinded in the receipt of that opinion that being Abraham's seed according to the flesh interested them in happiness and eternal life.

Fourthly, this opinion destroys the doctrine of the new covenant, and the nature of it, and the manner of God's making of it with the soul. For to make a new covenant with the soul is to write the law of God in a man's heart, and in his mind, and to infuse saving knowledge and faith, by which God unites the soul to himself, and so pardons all his sins, and without any condition considered in the creature, binds over himself to be their God freely in Christ, and binds over himself to own them to be his people. And only thus, and no otherwise, is God said to make his new covenant with a poor soul, whereas this dream would seem to bear you in hand that a whole nation may be in a new covenant, and have it made with them, and yet have none of all this work wrought in their hearts.

Fifthly, this opinion destroys the doctrine of justification by faith in Christ, only seeing that it doth hold out another way than by faith to come to justification, which is by carnal birth of believing parents. For if a soul be admitted into a covenant of life, I hope you are not ignorant that justification is a great privilege in the new covenant, and really the portion of all that are in that covenant.

Sixthly, this opinion destroys the doctrine and foundation of all gospel churches where it is held, which will appear by two things.

First, it destroys the matter of the church. You know that this is a fundamental truth, that the matter of the church ought, now under the gospel, to be "saints by calling";[64] "spiritual worshippers";[65] "lively stones";[66] "such as are redeemed from their vain conversation";[67] "such brought out of darkness into his marvelous light."[68]

Now this error destroys the truth, or opposeth itself against the truth of God, lying in all these Scriptures. It brings in the nation of believers, all born of their body, their seed's seed in their generation, if you will be faithful to this principle, whereon this seems to be grounded. For the covenant of circumcision was not only to the next generation immediately flowing from Abraham, "But to thy seed after thee in their generations."[69] And we see in

[64] 1 Cor. 1:2.
[65] John 4:23.
[66] 1 Pet. 2:5.
[67] 1 Pet. 1:18.
[68] 1 Pet. 2:9.
[69] [Gen. 17:9.]

that generation in Christ's time, they were as well called Abraham's seed, as Isaac himself was, and they did call Abraham their father.

Therefore, if the covenant of circumcision shall be man's pattern, we must necessarily have a church that is national, consisting of succeeding generations for many hundred years, coming out of believing person's loins, and so set up the partition wall again between the natural branches and those that are wild by nature. So that this tenet doth, of necessity, destroy the true matter of a church, because it unavoidably admits into the church all the unconverted and unregenerate children, born of the bodies of such persons that either are, or have been, accounted believers.

And as it destroys the matter of a church in admitting such that are not made disciples, so it occasions such as do believe, remaining in that opinion, to live in that sin of neglect of the Lord's baptism, contenting themselves with that counterfeit of baptism which they had in their infancy. So that this evil opinion occasions the constitution of a church or congregation of good and bad promiscuously, and all these unbaptized, both the good and the bad. And what light in the gospel have you to justify such an assembly to be the true church of Christ, that doth consist of some religious people, in the judgement of charity, and a world of carnal children admitted and received in among them, and all, both the carnal and the religious, never baptized with the Lord's baptism?

I do deny such an assembly can be owned an orderly church of Christ. Thus, you see what a great error this is that opposeth itself against so many fundamental points of the gospel.

QUESTION

But may some say, "Though we receive in children by baptism into our church, we do not admit them unto the supper."

ANSWER. The question is, when will you admit them? See what an untrodden path you are run into. Do you own your children to be in a covenant of grace and eternal life, and enrighted into the privileges of the same? And is baptism the privilege of the new covenant, and not the supper also? If it be, how dare you keep them from their right and privilege, I pray you? How long did the apostles baptize their members before they admitted them to the supper?

If you look in Acts 2:41–42, you shall find so many as gladly received the word of God were baptized, and presently they continued in the apostles' doctrine, fellowship, breaking of bread, and prayer, as soon as they were baptized.

Therefore, you have no ground at all, upon any pretense, to suspend such members that you own privileged in all the ordinances of God from the supper, which you have received into your church by your supposed baptism. Thus, you may see what horrible consequences flow naturally from maintaining a covenant of eternal life in the flesh.

Seventhly, this opinion defends another gross error, that persons may have right to a covenant of life without union or in being in Christ by faith. It is a sad thing that souls that profess knowledge in the gospel, and to be preachers of the same, should be so blinded thus to mislead people in so weighty a point as this is, and that should endeavour to leaven thousands of poor people with such a sad error that opposeth itself against the very substance of the gospel, in holding all the whole nation of Israel to be in a covenant of eternal life, and also the carnal children of believing parents among the Gentiles, though they had no union by faith in Christ, the greatest part of them.

III. NONE BUT BELIEVERS EVER HAD A RIGHT
TO THE COVENANT OF GRACE

I come to the third thing, which is to prove that the covenant of eternal life never was, nor shall be, made with any, but such as believe, or such as are in Christ. And for the better clearing of that, you must understand that as soon as the seed of the woman was promised, to wit, Christ Jesus—which was the whole of the new covenant, all promises being yea and amen, and spiritual and heavenly blessings being given in him, this being one main point then to be made known to the sons of men—that he must come out of the woman. You must, I say, understand that the Lord did presently make an outward covenant, which was typically entailed upon the flesh out of, which the Messiah should come.

But I must confess, this is not held forth so clearly till the time of Abraham, nor then so clear as it was afterwards by the hands of Moses. But it is clear to me that, in substance, the same covenant of ceremonial obedience which was given to Moses when the people came out of Egypt, the same was given to Adam's generation upon the promise of Christ, which was to go on in the fleshly line, out of which Christ was to come, and this to continue till he did come in the flesh, and then to cease. The reason that induceth me thus to judge is this.

I find Cain and Abel at the end of the year of days bring their sacrifice. And the one brought the firstlings of the flock, and the fat thereof. Thus, did God command the same things to Israel by Moses.[70] And you see Cain brought the firstfruits of the ground. And we find this delivered by Moses as part of the covenant to the Jews in Deuteronomy 8:4 and 26:2. For saith the Lord, "Thou shalt take of the first of all the fruit of the earth, which thou shalt bring of thy land that the LORD thy God giveth thee."[71]

Though ye do not here see from what rule Cain and Abel did thus do, yet we must take for granted they had it from God. How else could Abel have performed his worship acceptably, if he had not a ground to do it by faith? And it is certain he did it in faith. Therefore, he had rule for the same.[72] And we find, that in that time, there was a distinction of clean and unclean beasts that went into the ark.

Now what *cleanness* or *uncleanness* is here meant is by virtue of a law, for certainly that law which God gave to forbid such beasts and creatures was that which made one clean, and not another. And this law was by Moses delivered in Leviticus 11, spoken of to Peter in Acts 10, "What God hath cleansed, that call not thou common."[73] And likewise, the eating blood is forbidden,[74] or flesh with the life thereof; the same Moses gave Leviticus 17:10–11, where blood is forbidden upon the same ground and reason.

We find that God hints at a sin of the old world for which he

---

[70] Exod. 13:12–13; 34:19.

[71] Mic. 7:1; Lev. 2:12, 14; Prov. 3:19.

[72] Heb. 11:4.

[73] Acts 10:15.

[74] Gen. 9:4.

brought the flood, which was that the sons of God married the daughters of men, seeing they were fair, which must needs be understood there was a law prohibiting Seth's posterity to marry with Cain's.[75] This law was also given by Moses in Deuteronomy 7:2–3. We must, of necessity, understand these laws were from God to Adam, and so to his sons. And so, in substance, the same was given to Abraham with some additions, and the same by Moses, committed to writing with further additions.

But this is the result that I would come to: God, having promised the seed of the woman to come out of that flesh, did institute an external covenant of worship that the Lord did carry all along upon the flesh, or line, out of which the Messiah should come, and in which flesh the Word would be incarnate. I understand upon the first promise of Christ to Adam and Eve, God then made this ceremonial covenant of worship with Adam's family. Therefore, both his sons were trained up as worshippers, and this must needs be, because Cain was never in a covenant of grace, nor do we have grounds to judge that he had ever any appearance of true grace in him. But God, having no intent to bring his promised seed out of Cain or Abel, and also resolved there should be a world as well as a church, he suffers Cain to murder Abel, upon which he rejects Cain with all his posterity as a fugitive and a vagabond. From what did he reject him but from this church covenant of ceremonial obedience and worship? But when Seth was born, God, as it appears to me, did renew a fresh election upon him and his seed according to the flesh. And the whole race of Seth were God's church. God hereby teaches that

---

[75] Gen. 6:5.

the Messiah must come out of that family according to the flesh, and not out of Cain's or his posterity, nor any other.

And when God had destroyed the world by the flood, then there was only Noah's family, consisting of eight persons, being all of them in this church covenant of worship for a time, till God pitched a fresh election upon Shem by the mouth of Noah, his father, where Ham and Japheth, with their posterities, are passed by, though as truly the seed of believing Noah as Shem was.[76] And this ceremonial covenant of works goes on upon Shem till the time of Abraham. The world growing then numerous, God would have his church in a more narrow compass, and more especially, take unto him that particular family out of which Christ should come, which was Abraham. So that, by the way, observe the main ground upon which God elects Abraham's family into the outward covenant with himself, and not Lot's, nor any of the rest of the godly families then living in the world.

It was not because Abraham was any more a believer, or his family the family of a believer. For if so, then Lot and his family, and all the godly men's families then in the world, had been necessarily taken into the covenant of circumcision, because they and their families had been believers as well as Abraham's. For this is a sure rule: if God gives a promise or a command to any person considered in such a capacity as a believer, then whosoever is a believer, that command and promise belongs unto them. I might, by manifold instances, clear this, as when God saith to Joshua, "I will not fail thee, nor forsake thee,"[77] this being not made to him under any other consideration, but as a believer.

[76] Gen 9:26.
[77] Josh. 1:5.

The apostle is bold to say this promise is made to the whole church of the Hebrews, they being all believers as Joshua was.[78] But this covenant of circumcision, now so termed, was made with Abraham, his seed and family, and not upon this ground—because he was a believer—but because Christ must come out of his flesh and line. Therefore, to confirm and ratify this to Abraham, that Christ should so come, and to point out to all the world where they must look for and expect the Christ, God doth as much as say, in Abraham's loins you must expect him, and nowhere else. For as Christ saith to the woman of Samaria, the Jews know what they worship, for salvation is of the Jews.[79] Therefore, to be sure, the covenant of worship runs in that line.

But now, Abraham had eight sons—the one by Sarah,[80] the other by Hagar,[81] and six sons by his wife Keturah,[82] to which he gave gifts and sent away to the east country from his son Isaac. And this covenant of works did belong only to Isaac and his seed, for when God had, in Genesis 11:7, 17 promised that he would be the God of Abraham and his seed in their generations, and give them Canaan, in the conclusion of this covenant he begins to speak to Abraham of a son he should have by Sarah, and that she should be the mother of nations.[83]

Abraham, being affected with his son Ishmael, which he then enjoyed, saith, "O that Ishmael might live in thy sight."[84] As if

---

[78] Heb. 13:5.
[79] [John 4:22.]
[80] Gen. 21:2.
[81] Gen. 16.
[82] Gen. 25:1, 26.
[83] Heb. 11.
[84] [Gen. 17:18.]

Abraham should say, Lord I understand that thou hast made a church covenant with me and my seed after me, taking my seed in their generations into external covenant with thee. O, as if he should say, that Ishmael might be the seed upon which this covenant might run. Where God tells Abraham that he had heard his prayer, that he would bless Ishmael with manifold outward blessings otherwise. But, saith he, my covenant shall be with Isaac, meaning here that outward covenant of circumcision where you have Ishmael and the six sons of Keturah, with all their posterity, passed by in this fresh election of Isaac and his seed, which were only elected in this covenant.

Therefore, the bond child and the six sons of Keturah, though as truly children of believers as Isaac was, yet they are all dismissed this covenant and privileges of the same.

The six sons by Keturah, as you have heard before, Abraham gave them gifts and sent them into the east country. And when Isaac had two sons in Rebecca's womb, God again made a fresh election of Jacob and his seed in their generations, passing by Esau and his seed. For, saith God, there are two nations in thee and two peoples. So he chose Jacob, considered as a nation, and passed by Esau, considered as another nation. For it is plain from those words there are two nations and two peoples, that the election was a national election and a national rejection. Ane he saith, "The elder shall serve the younger."[85] This saying, the elder shall serve the younger, is interpreted by Malachi 1 to be a loving of Jacob and a hating of Esau, laying his mountain waste—that is his church power or privilege that he seemingly had expected to

---

[85] [Gen. 25:23.]

82

have been heir of—and the loving of Jacob is meant the external electing love into the covenant of circumcision, according to that in Deuteronomy 7:7–8. Speaking there of the whole nation, "The LORD did not set his love upon you, nor choose you, because ye were more in number than any people; for ye were the fewest of all people: But because the LORD loved you."

This election and this love is equal alike to the whole nation of Israel. Therefore, so considered, you must mind this is, as I said before, only an external election of Jacob, and these in his lines, into the national covenant of circumcision, as before in Genesis 18. He saith, "In Isaac shall thy seed be called."[86] The meaning, as the 17th chapter expounds, is this: that the seed in their generations that God would continue the covenant of circumcision upon was that seed which was to come out of Isaac, and not that which came out of Ishmael, and the six sons of Keturah; none of them or their seed were to be of that great nation which God promised to make of Abraham. For the Lord saith to Abraham, "I will make a mighty nation of thee."[87]

Now by this nation, you must understand, is meant the national church taken into the covenant of circumcision, whereas in the spiritual covenant all the nations were to be blest in him, and he is to be the father of multitudes of nations.[88] But this covenant of circumcision must not relate to any but to those that came out of Isaac, with his family, and then those that came out of the loins of Jacob, with his family, though this be a true literal interpretation of these texts, and really the proper mind of God.

---

[86] [Gen. 21:12.]
[87] Gen. 18:18.
[88] Gen. 12:3; 17:4–5.

Yet, there is a mystical and spiritual sense pointed and driven at, which Paul, that infallible apostle, did clearly give out from those texts in Romans 9. That as Isaac typed out Christ, so this temporal seed elected in Isaac typed out this spiritual election in Christ. The temporal seed in a temporal covenant, elected in Jacob, points out the choice of Christ and all his seed into a spiritual covenant.

So a spiritual election, in these texts, was typed and figured out, as the apostle doth clearly maintain—the apostles not being the ministers of the letter, but the Spirit.[89] But most true it is that Jacob and the whole nation in him were elected into an outward covenant, and Esau and his seed were not, but were refused and passed by. And consider, now, in the womb, was Jacob and his posterity any more the seed of a believer than Esau and his seed were? Sure it is [that] he was not. Therefore, away with that error taken for granted that the covenant of circumcision was made to believers and their seed.

This covenant of circumcision, you may clearly see, was not made to Abraham, nor to his seed considered as a believers, but upon this ground or reason that the Messiah was to come of Abraham, not of Lot. The Messiah was to come out of Isaac and not of Ishmael, nor of the six sons of Keturah. And Christ was to come out of Jacob and his posterity, and not out of Esau. Here you may nakedly see how greatly they mistake that think the covenant was made to Abraham and his seed considered as believers and believers' seed.

If a national covenant was made with Abraham and his seed

---

[89] 2 Cor. 3.

according to the flesh, out of which flesh the Messiah was to come, and that upon this reason then you cannot conclude that the covenant can belong to any Gentile and his seed but upon the same ground, therefore, if you would tell where to find a Gentile, now, among many others that were to have Christ to come out of his loins according to the flesh, then you would have the same ground to say that, in like manner, a church covenant should run upon him and his seed, until Christ were come out of that flesh or line.

But when Christ was come and fully exhibited in the flesh, then the ground upon which this covenant was given being ceased, the covenant also ceaseth. Therefore, for any man to go about to defend a covenant in the flesh, it is a doctrine virtually denying that Christ is come and fully manifested in the flesh.

OBJECTION

Therefore, you may from all that hath been spoken draw this conclusion: that there was never a covenant of eternal life made with any but with such as did and do believe, all along till Christ, not since.

ANSWER. Therefore, see that objection answered that the spiritual privileges are not less under the gospel than under the law, though we deny all the carnal generation to have any right to the covenant of grace or privileges thereof. Both then as well as now, the offers and tenders of the gospel, we must confess, were to that nation, and in that sense they were called the children of the prophets and of the covenant.[90] And in that respect, now the privileges are larger because all nations are, in the same sense, the children of the prophets and of the covenant, now since Christ came, the prophet and minister of God, having commission now to publish the gospel or new covenant to all nations.

But further, to prove that none have [a] right to the covenant of grace or life but such as had and have union with Christ by faith, is most plain.

First, because as you have heard the new covenant was confirmed of God in Christ only.[91] And all the promises are in Christ yea and amen.

Therefore, this covenant cannot belong to any soul out of Christ because they are yea and amen in him.[92] "This cup *is* the new testament in my blood," saith Christ.[93] If the New Testament be in Christ's blood, then what hath any carnal or unbelieving wretch to do with this testament, that have not faith in his blood?

And further, we do find in Matthew 3:17 the Lord saith, "This is my beloved Son, in whom I am well pleased." Mark the words, "in whom." Then to be sur, *out of him*, he is not well pleased—that is, in respect to this especial well-pleasedness, or electing love in the covenant of life, according to that in Ephesians 1:6. He hath made us accepted in the Beloved; out of the Beloved there can be no acceptation. Therefore, it is said God accepted Abel and his offering.[94] The author to the Hebrews, chapter 11:4, tells you, "By

---

[90] Acts 3 and latter end.
[91] Gal. 3:17.
[92] 1 Cor. 11:25.
[93] [Luke 22:20.]
[94] Gen. 4:4.

faith Abel offered unto God a more excellent sacrifice than Cain, by which he obtained witness that he was righteous." So, by faith in the promised seed he came to be righteous and accepted of God. As you have heard in Ephesians 1:3, God hath blest us with all spiritual and heavenly blessings in heavenly things in Christ Jesus. Therefore, no heavenly or spiritual blessing can belong to any out of Christ. "For as in Adam all die, even so in Christ shall all be made alive."[95] There is none made alive, but those that are in Christ, for the wicked men's resurrection is not said to be to life, but to damnation.[96] And therefore, in thee shall all the nations of the earth be blessed,[97] must imply thus much, that out of Christ, the true seed, all the nations should be accursed.[98]

I must confess, it is a sad thing that at such a time of the world as this, where the means of grace and knowledge of the gospel hath been so plentifully held forth, that we must be forced to bestow such pains to prove that men cannot be in a state of salvation and acceptation before God in a covenant of grace without union in Christ by faith. But howsoever, consider that the apostle saith there is no other name under heaven by which we can be saved, but by the name of Jesus, and a particular faith in him.[99] And therefore, Peter saith in John 6:68, "Lord, to whom shall we go? thou hast the words of eternal life." He is the way, the truth, and the life.[100] There is none [who] can come into the Father's love and mercy, nor into the covenant of life, or any spiritual privi-

---

[95] [1 Cor. 15:22.]

[96] 1 Cor. 15:21; John 5:28–29.

[97] Gen. 18:18.

[98] Gen. 12:3 with 22:18; Gal. 3:8.

[99] Acts 4:12.

[100] John 14:6.

lege, but by him. He is the narrow way that leads to life, and few there be that find it.[101] Therefore, saith the apostle, "He that hath the Son hath life; and he that hath not the Son of God hath not life."[102] But all the carnal, unbelieving children, from the foundation of the world unto this day, have not Christ, therefore not life—that is to say nor the covenant of life, nor the justification of life, which every man must needs have that is in that covenant of life. We find that all the patriarchs and holy men of God, by faith and patience, inherited the promises, and not by generation.[103] Therefore, sprang there even of one, and him as good as dead, so many as the stars in the sky for multitude, and as the sand which is by the seashore, innumerable; these all died in faith.

This text speaks of that spiritual and believing seed of Abraham which he considered as believing and faithful. Abraham was the father of [them], according to Genesis 15:5–6, "So shall thy seed be."

Secondly, it further appears that the covenant of eternal life was never made with any but such as believe, because all unbelievers both of Jews and Gentiles are charged under sin and have the wrath of God abiding on them.[104] Yea, though of the seed of Israel and children of that covenant of circumcision, to them Christ saith, "If ye believe not that I am he, ye shall die in your sins."[105] And the gospel tells the national church of the Jews that those of them that believed not were condemned already, be-

---

[101] Matt. 7:14.
[102] 1 John 5:12.
[103] Heb. 6:12; 11:12.
[104] John 3:36; Rom. 3:9.
[105] John 8:24.

cause they believed not in the only begotten Son of God,[106] which clearly proves that none of them were in a covenant of life by generation. For if they had, then the want of conversion would not have damned them, nor left them in a state of damnation.

Further, doth not Christ himself call and account the unbelieving Jews the world when he saith to his disciples, "If ye were of the world, the world would love his own: but because ye are not of the world, but I have chosen you out of the world, therefore the world hateth you"?[107] And this world that Christ chooseth his disciples out of, and that hated his disciples as they had formerly hated him, are but the nation of the Jews that were in that covenant of circumcision, which plainly proves that all unbelievers in that nation were the world, and therefore not in a covenant of grace.

And again, it must needs be so, because the apostle saith in Romans 4:16, "Therefore it is of faith, that it might be by grace; to the end the promise might be sure to all the seed."

Observe from the text, if the promise, or covenant, or any spiritual privilege, should be entailed upon the flesh, or conveyed any way then by faith, it could not be by grace.

And again, faith is the first differencing grace to difference God's people from all other, and put no difference between us and them, purifying their hearts by faith.[108] Therefore, it is impossible the covenant of grace can be made to any other but such as have faith. And again, I find none counted the spiritual seed of Abraham, unto whom the covenant of life belongs, but them that

---

[106] John 3:18.
[107] [John 15:19.]
[108] Acts 15:9.

are in Christ by faith, as Galatians 3:28–29, "There is neither Jew nor Greek, there is neither bond nor free, there is neither male nor female: for ye are all one in Christ Jesus. And if ye be Christ's, then are ye Abraham's seed, and heirs according to the promise." And so, Romans 4:14, "For if they which are of the law be heirs, faith is made void, and the promise made of none effect," meaning, thereby, the covenant of circumcision, as appears in verse 10 and 11. And so, in Romans 9:7–8, "Neither, because they are the seed of Abraham, are they all children: but, In Isaac shall thy seed be called. That is, they which are the children of the flesh, these are not the children of God: but the children of the promise are counted for the seed."

Where you see that the apostle doth deny that seed of Abraham, that were only his children according to the flesh, to be the spiritual seed, but such as are born of promise, or begotten by promise, they are accounted for the seed chosen in him, and united to him by faith.

These were pointed and figured out by the national and temporal seed that came out of the loins of Isaac. Those souls there born in the house and bought with money were in the outward covenant and privileges, but these regenerate and born again by promise are the heavenly seed. So the heavenly generation are such only born from above, and this is that the psalmist speaks of in Psalm 22:30, "A seed shall serve him; it shall be accounted to the Lord for a generation."

For the temporal Israel, and the typical election of them into the temporal covenant, did point out this spiritual election in a spiritual covenant, confirmed of God in Christ Jesus.

Further, it appears that none, but such as believe, are in a covenant of grace because without faith it is impossible to please God.[109] Therefore, Abel, by faith, had his person and his offering accepted, but Cain and his offering being not in faith, God accepted not.[110] For all the thoughts of such a man are only evil, and that continually till they believe.[111] All the imaginations of all believers, till converted, are evil, and only evil continually.

Secondly, their words are evil.

> O generation of vipers, how can ye, being evil, speak good things? for out of the abundance of the heart the mouth speaketh. A good man out of the good treasure of the heart bringeth forth good things: and an evil man out of the evil treasure bringeth forth evil things.[112]

And as their thoughts and words are evil, so in like manner their actions are all evil, natural actions, as eating. "When he is about to fill his belly, God shall cast the fury of his wrath upon him, and shall rain it upon him while he is eating."[113] Thus, you see, natural actions are evil, such as eating and drinking for satisfying his hunger, and also civil actions are evil, as Proverbs 21:4, "An high look, and a proud heart, and the plowing of the wicked, is sin." If plowing, then all his civil actions, and also his best duties of worship, as his sacrifice, is an abomination to God.[114] Upon this ground, it must needs be that the covenant of grace and eternal life cannot belong to any such persons that do not

---

[109] Heb. 11:6.
[110] Gen. 4:4
[111] Gen. 6:5; 8:21.
[112] Matt. 12:34–35.
[113] Job 20:23.
[114] Prov. 28:9; 15:8; Isa. 1; 66.4.

believe, for it is impossible to be in a covenant of grace, and yet not to have persons, nor any of their best actions, accepted.

Yea further, all mankind are compared to beasts till they believe. "For vain men would be wise, though man be born like a wild ass's colt."[115] Yea the Lord saith in Revelation 21:8 that the fearful, and unbelieving, and the abominable, and murderers, and whoremongers, and sorcerers, and idolaters, and all liars, shall have their portion in the lake, which burneth with fire and brimstone, which is the second death.

Beloved, therefore, if any have been so deluded as to believe such a notorious error as this is, to think that any ever hath been in the covenant of life but such as are in Christ by faith, I desire God may give you repentance for maintaining such a fundamental error as this is.

IV. ANSWERS TO SCRIPTURES ALLEGED TO PROVE INFANT BAPTISM

And now, in the fourth place, I shall endeavour to answer such Scripture allegations, and those especially brought in from the New Testament, to countenance this error, wherein I shall endeavour to take off those false and corrupt glosses that are usually put upon them, wherein men pretend to prove the covenant of grace among the Gentiles to run in the flesh and line of believing parents under the gospel, which I am sure was never yet, since the world began, nor never shall be with any, neither parents nor children, but such individual persons that particularly believed in Christ with their own hearts.

---

[115] Job 11:12; cf. Jer. 2:23–24.

ACTS 2:39

And first let me speak to that in Acts 2:39, which is usually pretended to be a proof of the covenant in the flesh. The words are these, "For the promise is unto you, and to your children, and to all that are afar off, even as many as the LORD our God shall call."

Now I pray you take notice how evident this text makes against this error. For this text affirms only the promises to belong to so many even as God shall call, and that is a fundamental truth, if by promise you understand the gift of the Holy Ghost, or remission of sins, or both, to be promised in this text.

It is most true, that so many as God shall call have an interest, both to Christ and all the promises in him, and only they, for saith the text, "Repent, and be baptized every one of you in the name of Jesus Christ for the remission of sins, and ye shall receive the gift of the Holy Ghost."[116] So that remission of sins and the gift of the Holy Ghost, it is safe to understand here to be meant that promise that is said to belong to them, to their children, and to those afar off, even so many of them, and their children, and of those afar off, as the Lord our God should call.

Agreeable to the words thus understood is Romans 8:30, "Moreover whom he did predestinate, them he also called: and whom he called, them he also justified: and whom he justified, them he also glorified." So that justification, or remission of sins, is here given only to called persons; with these agreeth that of Hebrews 9:15, "And for this cause he is the mediator of the new testament, that by means of death, for the redemption of the

---

[116] [Acts 2:38.]

transgressions that were under the first testament, they which are called might receive the promise of eternal inheritance." So here, you see, that those that are predestinated to have a covenant of life, and the blessing given in that covenant, are first called. "He hath called us out of darkness into his marvelous light."[117]

Now this text is plain to prove that those Jews and proselytes that then heard him, and their children, and also the ten tribes now afar off, and also the Gentiles, the promises did belong to so many of all these as God should call, and except souls be given up to a spirit of delusion, will any dare to affirm that the promises of the Spirit, remission of sins and eternal life, do belong to any other? Will any be so ignorant as to judge that those promises did belong to the generation of the Jews whether they were called or not, though they continued in unbelief and hardness of heart and impenitency? Is not such a corrupt interpretation against Christ's words to that very people? "If ye believe not that I am he, ye shall die in your sins," speaking to these very Jews.[118] And doth not John the Baptist say to these, "He that believeth not the Son shall not see life; but the wrath of God abideth on him"?[119] [He was] directing this speech indefinitely to the generation of the Jews, the seed of Abraham, such as were in the covenant of circumcision.

But if by the children you understand so many of them as God should call, whether then at that time or afterwards to the end of the world, it is most true that to such of their children the promise of grace did belong.

But beloved, the Scripture is in nothing more full than in this,

---

[117] 1 Pet. 2:9.
[118] John 8:24.
[119] John 3:36.

that the promise of grace belonged not to any of those Jew's seed, but such as were called. For God shuts them under unbelief, and because of unbelief they were broken off.[120] If unbelief excluded them from that external relation, which before Christ's death they then had in the covenant entailed on the flesh, and Christ coming in the flesh, and fully exhibiting and putting an end to that covenant, no other covenant standing in force in the church of God, but what Christ was the mediator of, these unbelieving Jews, of necessity, were broken off. The promise of remission of sins was so far from running upon the unbelieving Jews, the true fleshly seed of Abraham, that the apostle Paul affirms the contrary, "But when divers were hardened, and believed not, but spake evil of that way before the multitude, he departed from them."[121] And,

> But when the Jews saw the multitudes, they were filled with envy, and spake against those things which were spoken by Paul, contradicting and blaspheming. Then Paul and Barnabas waxed bold, and said, It was necessary that the word of God should first have been spoken to you: but seeing ye put it from you, and judge yourselves unworthy of everlasting life, lo, we turn to the Gentiles. For so hath the Lord commanded us.[122]

And verses 50–51, "But the Jews stirred up the devout and honourable women, and the chief men of the city, and raised persecution against Paul and Barnabas, and expelled them out of their coasts. But they shook off the dust of their feet against them."

---

[120] Rom. 11.

[121] Acts 19:9.

[122] Acts 13:45–47.

And therefore, Paul is plain in Romans 11, saying that God had a certain number that were of the eternal election among the Jews. Those obtained [a] right to the remission of sins, and the rest were blinded and hardened. But it should seem to be the general understanding of those that urge this text for a covenant in the flesh, that if they were the seed of the Jews, though they were not called, nor did not believe, but were hardened in their continuance in unbelief, yet this promise of remission of sins, and the gift of the Holy Ghost, belongs to them. And this interpretation, that this text must have to defend a covenant in the flesh, which I leave to any intelligent man to consider, how greatly erroneous it is to affirm that the promise of the remission of sins belongs to the unbelieving and hardened children of the Jews, that God hath, nor doth, call, so that you may clearly see that the truth lies in this text, that the promise is to no more of fathers nor children, nor those afar off but such as God by his especial grace doth call to be the sons of God by faith.

1 CORINTHIANS 7:14

Another Scripture made use of, or rather abused and wrested to defend this error, is 1 Corinthians 7:14. "For the unbelieving husband is sanctified by the wife, and the unbelieving wife is sanctified by the husband: else were your children unclean; but now are they holy." Whence is gathered, by those of that opinion, that this holiness is, as they call it, a federal holiness, of a covenant holiness, that is to say, God, having taken the believing parent with the child into covenant with himself, the child is, in this sense, holy—that is covenant holy.

Now for the better understanding [of] this text, I pray, consider how, and in what sense, God takes persons into covenant with himself. And that, as you have heard, is two ways. Either he takes souls to himself in a typical covenant, so he took Israel to himself in that covenant, and in that sense they may be said to be separated from the rest of the world, which separation of them from the rest of the world to himself is a holiness that the carnal Jew was only partaker of, such a typical and legal holiness that people being separated from all other nations in the world to God in this covenant. Now the word *holy* signifies so much as separating or setting apart, and in this sense the vessels of the temple were holy, as also the priests, being by law set apart from the rest of Israel to offer the bread of their God.

Now in the second place, there is also a new covenant, or a covenant of life, that God takes a people to himself, which is to write his law in their hearts and in their minds, to sanctify them, to justify them. Now this internal holiness, which God, as an effect of that covenant, infuseth into the heart, is only this new covenant holiness, for there is no other holiness that relates to the new covenant, when the heart and the inward man shall be purified through faith. And when the whole heart and affections are, by the powerful work of God's grace, separated from sin, and those vanities below to heaven and heavenly things, this is the only holiness that the covenant of eternal life conveys to souls. The hypocrite may have this in appearance, but the elect and chosen have this only in truth. He puts no difference between us and them, purifying their hearts by faith. And he hath, by one offering, for ever perfected them that are sanctified.[123] This sanctification of the Spirit, and belief of the truth, goes always together.[124] Therefore, it is impossible that this should be the meaning of the text, that all believers' carnal seed are in a covenant of eternal life, and so have their hearts purified and sanctified through the work of the Spirit and faith before they are born, and in this sense, are born holy.

I know no other sanctification the Scripture speaks of, belonging to a covenant of grace and eternal life. And for that external or typical holiness in an outward covenant, it cannot be, because that was abolished through Christ's death, as appears in Hebrews chapters 8 and 9. Therefore, far be it from the apostle to intend here the countenancing of any such erronious opinion, as that every believers' child was, by virtue of his first birth, internally holy with that holiness of truth, as the apostle calls it.[125]

If you please, therefore, hearken to the true meaning of this text, which is to this effect: the Corinthians, having sent several doubts and questions to the apostle to resolve and answer, as appears in the 1st verse of this chapter, he answereth them particularly, and it seems among the rest they had a Jewish question started, grounded, as we suppose, upon Ezra 9 and Deuteronomy 7:2, where you find it was unlawful for a Jew to marry with a stranger. Therefore, Ezra caused all those men that had taken them strange wives to put them away as not lawfully married, because contrary and against the law [they were] given to them. Therefore, they were to put them away, and the children born of

---

[123] Heb. 10. [Heb. 10:14.]
[124] 2 Thess. 2:13.
[125] Eph. 4:24.

them as illegitimate and unclean in an unlawful fellowship.

These Corinthians, it seems, did propound in writing to the apostle this question, whether such of them as had unbelieving husbands and wives, yet remaining in idolatry, might lawfully abide with them in that fellowship in the marriage bed, and whether that fellowship were not unclean and unlawful as in Ezra's time.

Unto this question the apostle answers [in] verse 12,

> But to the rest speak I, not the Lord: If any brother hath a wife that believeth not, and she be pleased to dwell with him, let him not put her away. And the woman which hath an husband that believeth not, and if he be pleased to dwell with her, let her not leave him.

But also, might they say, "Why is not our marriage fellowship unclean?" Therefore, in verse 14, saith he, "The unbelieving wife is sanctified." As the Geneva Translation hath it, "to the believing husband, or else were your children unclean, but now are they holy." As if Paul should say, the reason why I would have the believing husband to abide with the unbelieving wife is this: because the unbeliever, now since the partition wall is down between Jew and Gentile, may justifiably be a wife to a believing husband, there being now no law in the New Testament against such marriages, especially considering their marriage was transacted when they were both idolatrous heathen.

Now, it being taken for granted their marriage was lawful in these words, "The unbelieving wife is sanctified to the believing husband," and that it be understood that the unbelieving husband is, by the law of marriage, sanctified to, or set apart or separated to, or made holy to the believing wife, the law of marriage having separated him from all other women in the world to be to her and her only, else were your children unclean. Mark, saith the apostle, "Else were your children unclean, but now are they holy." That is, if the law of God did not set the unbeliever apart to the believer, and so justify their fellowship in the marriage bed, then would the children begotten in that fellowship be unclean and base-born, but now they are holy, that is now they are begotten in holy wedlock, according to the holy law of marriage, not as those children were in Ezra's time which were unclean.

So that from the unbelievers lawful and sanctified abode with the believer doth the apostle conclude the children to be clean or holy. And thus, all children of heathen are in the same sense holy, that are begotten in holy wedlock. For as the fellowship of man and woman in the bed, being not according to the law, is called fornication, uncleanness, and unholiness, so the fellowship of any two persons, even of heathen, being according to that law of marriage, it is then clean or holy, and so the children begotten in that fellowship are said to be clean or holy begotten. But there was none [who] doubted of the holiness of the heathen, they never having any law to prohibit their marriage together. But now the Jews having an express law against marrying with any other nation, it was legally unclean or unholy to match with any such, or to bed with any such that were not Jews or proselytes.

Now that law, you must mind, was part of the partition wall between Jew and Gentile, which is abolished since Christ's full exhibition. So then, take the sense of the text thus.

That first, the apostle bids the believers continue with the unbelievers or idolaters.

Secondly, adding this reason, because their fellowship is holy.

Thirdly, from an absurdity, which would else follow, and that is, "Else were your children unclean, but now are they holy."

ROMANS 11:16–17

In the next place, let us speak to that in Romans 11:16–17, made use of by some to prove a covenant of eternal life in the flesh. The words are these, "For if the firstfruit be holy, the lump is also holy: and if the root be holy, so are the branches. And if some of the branches be broken off, and thou, being a wild olive tree, wert grafted in among them, and with them partakest of the root and fatness of the olive tree."

The usual exposition is that this root is Abraham, and these firstfruits are Abraham, Isaac, and Jacob, and these branches are to be understood [as] the body of Israel that came of their loins, as the root and the branches. And so, the Jews, through unbelief, with their generation, were broken off, and so also the Gentiles, with their generation and seed, are brought in. This last clause, which mainly serves for their purpose, they bring in by head and shoulders that the Gentile and his seed is brought in. What is there in that text which will countenance that clause, if it be truly examined?

But let us consider this text, and see what it will afford to prove a covenant of eternal life, to life, to run in the flesh of believing Gentiles, for that is it the text must prove, without the which in vain it is alleged. And for the better examining of the same, we will take for granted that by *root* is meant Abraham, and by *first-*

fruits is meant Abraham, Isaac, and Jacob, which are spoken of. If so, then you must, of necessity, distinguish Abraham, as the apostle doth, as begetting and working Abraham and as believing and faithful Abraham. And so, thus you must understand Abraham in a twofold covenant, as hath been before cleared. Wherein he was in a double sense holy. As he was in that absolute covenant of grace, so considered, he was spiritually holy. And considered as in the covenant of works, that conditional covenant made with him, he was legally holy.

Now, all the nation of the Jews, being separated by God from all other nations in and by the same covenant, are in this sense holy as Abraham was. And as he was holy in a covenant of life with a spiritual holiness, so only those of the spiritual and believing seed, as his branches in that sense, can be said to be holy. And the like may be said of these patriarchs who as the firstfruits.

Consider them in the spiritual covenant. So they, as the firstfruits, may be said to be spiritually holy. So, by the lump, you must understand that seed, in that covenant, to be only spiritually holy, as the firstfruits were. But if you consider them in the covenant of works, the external national covenant, as the firstfruit in that covenant were legally holy so were the whole lump, that is the whole nation of the Jews thus holy, till that covenant was abolished and put an end to. And then, this covenant entailed on the flesh of Abraham being put an end to or abolished, it must needs be that the branches must be broken off, namely, such as, only by nature or birth, had an interest to that covenant, or joining only to the family.

And the distinctions of the covenants and seeds being here

observed, it will enlighten the soul to understand [that in] this place we find this distinction carried on in the beginning of the chapter, namely, two covenants and two seeds, and both in the church of Israel, such as some would call the covenanting seed. There were two seeds amongst the external covenanting seed; there was the covenant of works and the covenant of grace.

As for example, the apostle speaks of the whole body of Israel, then of a select number out of Israel, which God foreknew, and therefore brings in the case of Elijah where God had in Israel 7,000 selected from the rest of the same body of Israel in the outward covenant with him.[126] And also, in the apostles' time, he saith that there were a select number, "according to the election of grace," which God had chose out of Israel.[127] Then saith he, "if by grace, then is it no more of works: otherwise grace is no more grace. But if it be of works, then it is no more grace: otherwise work is no more work,"[128] where you hear the apostle clearly distinguisheth two seeds in Israel as two covenants—the one a conditional covenant of works, the other of grace, an absolute covenant, as in the verses 4–7 of that 11th chapter of the Romans.

And so, the main drift here of the apostle is to hold forth that though God did now cast off the carnal seed from being his church that were only in the covenant of works—this covenant standing no longer in force, but growing old and vanishing away, as in Hebrews 8:13, in which covenant he chose this nation to himself—yet nevertheless, the apostle doth affirm that God had a remnant that were elect that should be called of that natural seed

---

[126] 1 Kgs. 19.

[127] [Rom. 11:5.]

[128] [Rom. 11:6.]

of Israel, even to the end, though for the present the greatest part were hardened in unbelief.

So that when he saith the branches were broken off, we are not to understand that such of them as related to Abraham as a father, or root of believers, in a covenant of grace were broken off. For then we should hold falling away from and out of a covenant of life, which would be a gross error. But the branches were broke off from the root considered in that national covenant of circumcision, which was a covenant of works that carnal people might really be in, as you heard before. This national covenant now ceasing, as I have shewed, and being put an end to by Christ, he becoming the substance of the same covenant, and that being the partition wall at that time between Jews and Gentiles.

But the apostle now affirms in Galatians 5:6 and 6:16, "For in Jesus Christ neither circumcision availeth any thing, nor uncircumcision; but faith which worketh by love." Therefore, all of the Jews that believed not ceased to be members of God's church, because now Abraham is no way considered as a father and a root in the gospel-church, but as faithful and believing Abraham in a covenant of eternal life. Therefore, unbelief now cuts off the nation of the Jews.

QUESTION

Why had not unbelief cut them off many hundred years before?

ANSWER. The answer is plain. For so long as the typical covenant of works stood in force, Israel, by being of that family or that generation, whether they had faith or no, or any appearance of grace or no, were interested in that covenant and in the privileges thereof.

But now, when Christ was fully exhibited in the flesh, and that covenant ceasing and the covenant of life now only remaining, it becomes so that only those branches and that lump of believers, the spiritual lump, only remain in the church whether Jews or Gentiles.

So that if you will seriously mind the scope and drift of the apostle, you shall see that the lump and the branches, here intended, must needs be holy because the firstfruits and root are holy, which is meant those of God's spiritual elect of the Jews that he would call to the end of the world, which sense is confirmed in the 28th verse. For saith the apostle, "As concerning the gospel, they are enemies for your sakes," meaning the Gentiles, "but as touching the election, they are beloved for the father's sakes."[129] Not as if God hated these rejected Jews for the sakes of these Gentiles properly, or loved a certain number of the Jews for their father's sake properly.

But thus, for the gospel's sake they became enemies, that is the gospel promise or covenant, having, as you have heard before, respect to all nations.[130]

Now this gospel covenant, being not capable to be divulged to all nations so long as this external electing love to the nation of the Jews was kept on foot in that covenant of circumcision, being a partition wall, therefore this bond of favour and friendship, being broken in this external covenant, they came to be enemies because of the accomplishment of the promises of the gospel to

[129] [Rom. 11:28.]
[130] Gen. 12:3; 22:18; Gal. 3:8.

the Gentiles, that those beloved elected of the Jews, and ten tribes even, are beloved for their father's sake, meaning for the promise sake, made to their fathers concerning their calling, which must needs be accomplished.[131] For they are the seed of the blessed of the Lord, and their offspring with them, meaning all such elected offspring, as this 11th chapter of the Romans speaks of the calling. For saith the text, "As touching the election, they were beloved for the father's sake." So that for the promise sake, made to their fathers, they shall, in time, be actually elected with an eternal electing love.

But to mind this Scripture further, it makes exceedingly against any fleshly covenant running in the fleshly line of the Gentiles because these words, in verses 20-24, do declare that the Gentiles came to be Abraham's spiritual seed, and so a branch of that stock, only by faith in Christ, that fat olive. "And if ye be Christ's, then are ye Abraham's seed, and heirs according to the promise."[132] And as it is said the Gentiles are grafted into this stock or root of Abraham contrary to nature, it must needs cut off such a conclusion as that all believing Gentiles seed shall come by nature into this stock, it being not only against the whole scope and drift of this place, but against the express words which saith the Gentiles are grafted in contrary to nature, and stand by faith and further that unbelief broke off the Jews.

Now this would be a strange riddle, in my judgement, first to conclude that the whole nation of the Jews were in a covenant of eternal life, and yet never had faith—no not so much as visibly for the greatest part of them.

[131] Isa. 65:23.
[132] Gal. 3:29.

Secondly, that they were broken off from a covenant of eternal life, and why? Because of unbelief. And yet, nevertheless, believing Gentiles [and] their unbelieving seed, in the midst of his unbelief, is grafted in.

This, in substance, is what is drawn from this text for proving a covenant in the flesh. But let any impartially judge how much a shame it would be to wrest Scripture so contrary to the scope and meaning. For this chapter shews that there were two seeds, two covenants—one of grace, or the gospel, the other of works, and that men could not obtain aright to this gospel covenant, but by virtue of election, and that merely of grace. The other covenant of works, and the fleshly seed in this covenant, were broke off, that is from any privilege coming from Abraham according to the flesh, that fleshly covenant being put an end to by Christ being come in the flesh. All unbelieving Jews, upon that ground, cease to be God's church, much more unbelieving Gentiles. For if unbelief broke off the Jew, be sure it will as effectually keep out the Gentile, as it is clear it doth, because they stand by faith only, and are grafted in contrary to nature. And it is said the Jew, if he abide not in unbelief, shall be grafted in again.

From all which it is plain that there is no other way now under the gospel to come into, or stand, in the house or church of God but by faith, neither for Jew nor Gentile. And so, far is the apostle free from concluding that the Gentiles come in by nature. He affirms the contrary, that he is grafted in contrary to nature, plainly holding forth that all both Jews and Gentiles, in a state of unbelief, were excluded from those privileges.

For, as before hath been proved, the ground upon which the

covenant of circumcision was made unto Abraham and his seed, according to the flesh, was not because he was a believer, but because Christ was to come of that line according to the flesh.

If you could find out any Gentile under the gospel out of which the Messiah should come according to the flesh, then there were the same reason and ground that an external typical covenant should run in his line or flesh till the Messiah were fully exhibited.

But I hope none will be such an antichrist so highly to deny Christ come in the flesh, seeing Paul saith, "Henceforth know we no man after the flesh." For saith he, "we have known Christ after the flesh, yet now henceforth know we him no more."[133]

Men were known, that is approved as privileged persons in God's church, by being in that covenant entailed in the flesh of Abraham, namely, that covenant of circumcision, but from henceforth we know no man, no not Christ himself should be minded as standing interested in that covenant, he being now known to be one receiving a more excellent ministry than the ministry of circumcision, a better covenant grounded upon better promises.[134] The following words confirm this exposition, "Therefore if any man be in Christ, he is a new creature: old things are passed away; behold, all things are become new."[135] Compared with Galatians 6:15, "circumcision availeth any thing." Therefore, we are not now to know men according to the flesh.

No, not Christ as come in the flesh circumcised and by virtue of that privileged in the church. But we are now to know him

---

[133] [2 Cor. 5:16.]
[134] Heb. 8:6–7.
[135] [2 Cor. 5:17.]

as fully exhibited, and, as before, a minister of a better covenant grounded upon better promises.

So that this 11th chapter of the Romans doth so little serve to countenance the covenant of eternal life to run in the flesh, that it exceedingly makes against it, cuts it up by the roots, affirming no other of the Gentiles or their seed to be grafted into this stock or root, but contrary to nature, which he expounds to be by faith.

Therefore, take the whole drift and scope of that place, and you shall have two seeds, two covenants, a certain select number out of those that were in the old covenant elected into the new covenant. The rest of all the body of Israel in that old covenant were blinded and hardened, and never obtained an interest into the new covenant.

And when Jesus Christ, the substance of the old covenant, was come, then that ceased. And now, but one covenant remains. The covenant of God's church is, of necessity, only believers, and spiritual seed now can remain in the church. Hereupon, all the unbelieving seed of Jews and Gentiles are utterly excluded out from the church and church privileges, which never was so long as an old external covenant stood in force.

1 CORINTHIANS 10:1–4

The next Scripture text brought in for [the] defense of the covenant in the flesh is 1 Corinthians 10:1–4,

> Moreover, brethren, I would not that ye should be igno-
> rant, how that all our fathers were under the cloud, and
> all passed through the sea; And were all baptized unto
> Moses in the cloud and in the sea; And did all eat the

same spiritual meat; And did all drink the same spiritual
drink: for they drank of that spiritual Rock that followed
them: and that Rock was Christ.

This is another Scripture which is made use of to prove a covenant of salvation to run in the flesh.

But beloved, the drift of the apostle here is, as it is throughout the Scripture, to give out the mystery and substance that shadows typed out to come, according to that in 2 Corinthians 3. We are "not of the letter, but of the spirit,"[136] meaning that the main thing which the apostles did hold forth in their ministry, when they had to do with types and shadows, was to set forth the substance or Spirit, or heavenly things that was pointed at, and so here.

Beloved, know this, that these were all types and ceremonies here spoke of, belonging to the carnal Jew. Therefore, saith the apostle, "They were all baptized unto Moses in the cloud and in the sea." He doth not say they were all baptized into Christ, but unto Moses, which is a main passage I would present to you.

You must understand Moses was a solemn type. He was a saviour to save them out of the land of Egypt, their present bondage, into Canaan. He was a mediator of that temporal covenant, and in this did Moses type out Christ.[137] The temporal covenant did type out the spiritual and heavenly covenant, and the temporal Israel did type out the spiritual Israel.

This temporal redemption of Israel out of Egypt into Canaan typed out the spiritual redemption from sin, bondage, the world, and devil into that heavenly Canaan.

The covenant that Moses was the mediator of, you have heard,

[136] [2 Cor. 3:6.]
[137] Gal. 3:19.

110

was the covenant of circumcision, which is before cleared to be a covenant of works, delivered in substance to Abraham, but after committed by writing to Moses—as Acts 15:1, where the teachers did command them to be circumcised and keep the law after the manner of Moses; compared with John 7:22, "Moses therefore gave unto you circumcision; (not because it is of Moses, but of the fathers.)"

In Acts 15:1, it is said by the false teachers that except they were circumcised after the manner of Moses, they could not be saved. Those teachers were of the same opinion with these in our days who hold that the covenant of circumcision was a covenant of life, and therefore concluded such persons out of it could not be saved. Their conclusion was, doubtless, answerable to the premises, for if that circumcision had been as they judged it, a covenant of eternal life, then out of it none could have been saved. Therefore, it is said in the 5th verse, "But there rose up certain of the sect of the Pharisees which believed, saying, That it was needful to circumcise them, and to command them to keep the law of Moses." And in the 10th verse it is said, "Now therefore why tempt ye God, to put a yoke upon the neck of the disciples, which neither our fathers nor we were able to bear?" Which was the covenant of circumcision. Which, on God's part, was the promise of the land of Canaan with all the good things thereof and the external privileges as protection and preservation. And on their parts, they were bound to keep the law. Therefore, you shall find that Ezra and Nehemiah entered into an oath and a curse with the people then to keep this covenant on their part, as that nation were bound to do.

111

And this was that covenant which the false teachers persuaded the Galatians to be a covenant of life, and that they could not be saved without it, which covenant the apostle Paul called the flesh in Galatians 3:3, meaning that covenant which God had established in their flesh "for an everlasting covenant," as he so calls it, "and my covenant shall be in your flesh for an everlasting covenant." Therefore, saith Paul in Romans 4:1, "What shall we say then that Abraham our father, as pertaining to the flesh, hath found?" If Abraham were justified by works? Mark his exposition of that covenant, "as pertaining to the flesh" to be a covenant of works, which in the 10th verse he clears to be circumcision in opposition to that gospel promise, which Abraham had before he was circumcised, and so he doth all along in that chapter. Herein the 3rd of Galatians he doth set the covenant of grace and that of works in opposition. The one he calls the Spirit, the other flesh, which he most evidently explains in chapter 5:1–3, where saith he, "Stand fast therefore in the liberty wherewith Christ hath made us free, and be not entangled again with the yoke of bondage."

Here observe, again, that he calls it as Peter doth, "a yoke of bondage," which is evident that they were set at freedom and liberty from as that which was abolished, and they [were] freed from as a yoke, which neither they, nor their fathers, were able to hear, as appears in Galatians 5:1–3, "Behold, I Paul say to you, that if ye be circumcised, Christ shall profit you nothing." Nay. In verse 3, "For I testify again to every man that is circumcised, that he is a debtor to do the whole law." And in verse 4, he sets it in opposition to the covenant of grace. And this is explained more in Galatians 6:12–13.

Now all this considered, you may clearly see the covenant of circumcision made to Abraham and his seed in their generation, that he would give them Canaan with the blessings thereof, and in that sense be their God, to protect, preserve, and externally to privilege them with the means of grace and tenders of the gospel, and the external blessings of Canaan, [was] upon [the] condition [that] they would be circumcised and keep the law.

All these things are typical—this deliverance out of Egypt typing out the deliverance out of hell. Temporal Israel, after the flesh, that were redeemed out of Egypt, typed out the spiritual Israel that were redeemed out of the spiritual bondage. And, as before hath been said, Moses then [was] a temporal redeemer, mediator, or saviour, [who] typed out Christ, the spiritual mediator and saviour. Therefore, in 1 Corinthians 10:6 the apostle tells us these were our figures or types.

So this being premised, we have the sense of the text here plain, that as the spiritual disciple or Israelite, when he believes and confesseth his faith, thereby shewing his interest in Jesus Christ, is baptized into Christ Jesus, the mediator of that covenant, which he is in by faith.

So the temporal Israel by birth, or being bought with money, or cohabitation in that family of Israel, coming to have a right to the covenant of circumcision whereof Moses was the mediator, they were likewise baptized unto Moses, in the cloud and in the sea, that being as real a confirmation to them of the temporal deliverance from Egypt into Canaan by the hand of Moses as our baptism is a confirmation to the spiritual Israel of their spiritual deliverance by Jesus their mediator from death and condemnation to eternal life.

And whereas the apostle calls that meat *spiritual* meat, and that drink *spiritual* drink, he here speaks figuratively, as before affirmed. Not that the manna eaten by the whole nation of Israel was in itself spiritual, but it was a figure of the spiritual bread. Therefore, Christ saith to the Jews in John 6:32–33, "Verily, verily, I say unto you, Moses gave you not that bread from heaven; but my Father giveth you the true bread from heaven." Observe that word *giveth*. Not *did give*, but *giveth*. "For the bread of God is he which cometh down from heaven, and giveth life unto the world."

And therefore, saith he, "My Father giveth you the true bread from heaven," that is, the substance of that shadow. And so, that rock was Christ, meaning a figure or type of Christ.

What is all this, beloved, to the proving of a covenant of life running in the flesh, either then or now, to the Gentiles under the gospel? See, it is clear that all these ordinances, as the apostle calls them "carnal ordinances,"[138] did type out, or figure out, spiritual and substantial things. For their sacrifices for sin typed out Christ, but they were not Christ. And their typical remissions, which they had by their sacrifice, that remission, I say, which the whole body of Israel had by offering up their sin offering, can be understood to be no other but typical.

A man might be under that typical remission, and yet be under the wrath of God and be damned. And a poor Gentile at the utmost part of the earth, believing as Rahab did in Canaan, as

---

[138] Heb. 9:10.

truly justified—though he had none of this typical remission, and none of these before mentioned figures. So that we conclude the whole nation of the Jews had not a covenant of eternal life in the flesh made unto them, though they had a temporal typical covenant, as I have all along called it, that is consisting of such laws and privileges that had not Christ in them, but did point at him to come. Therefore, they are called in Hebrews 9, "Patterns of heavenly things," but not the very things themselves. They are called by the apostle beggarly elements,[139] or rudiments of the world,[140] or a schoolmaster to lead to Christ.[141] The Jews literal obedience to the law typed out the obedience to faith.[142]

Now, beloved, the literal obedience in itself performed by the carnal Jew, though it figured out the substantial obedience, namely, faith in Christ, and though the rest in Canaan typed out the spiritual rest in Christ, yet I hope no man will be so absurd, but he will confess, that this literal obedience was not the spiritual obedience, and that this rest in Canaan was but a shadow of that rest in Christ, not the very rest itself.

But some may say so of baptism and the supper, that these are the signs of inward and spiritual things, but it doth not follow that these are the spiritual things.

Beloved, observe warily, for here lies the ground of this great mistake—the want of distinguishing between these figures that type out Christ to come and these sacramental signs that do confirm and ratify his being already come.

---

[139] [Gal. 4:9.]

[140] [Col. 2:8.]

[141] [Gal. 3:24.]

[142] Deut. 30:12–24; Rom. 10:6–10.

Those typical signs and figures, then, which typed out Christ to come, did properly belong to that typical seed, the body of Israel that typed out the spiritual seed to come.

But now these signs, I say, these sacramental signs that are instituted since Christ came for the confirming he is come, these belong only to the spiritual seed in whom Christ is come already, dwelling in their hearts by faith.

Therefore, as Christ is a spiritual and substantial mediator of a substantial and spiritual covenant, so these spiritual administrations of the spiritual covenant belong only to such as are in Christ, and this new covenant by faith, and that have Christ dwelling in them, as hath been before in the former part of my discourse manifested.

In the New Testament, faith and repentance are required of them that are to be baptized. "See, here is water; what doth hinder me to be baptized? And Philip said, If thou believest with all thine heart, thou mayest,"[143] implying it was unlawful to baptize any that did not believe with all their heart, at least in profession. And so, when Christ dispenseth the supper, he commands it to be received by his disciples. He saith to his disciples, "Take, eat."[144] And he said to his disciples, "Drink ye all of it."[145] And Paul saith, "But let a man examine himself, and so let him eat of that bread, and drink of that cup."[146]

If you will not shut your eyes against the light, there is nothing more plain than this: that those administrations, under the

---

[143] Acts 8:36–37.
[144] Matt. 26:26.
[145] Matt. 26:27.
[146] [1 Cor. 11:28.]

116

old covenant, did not require such qualifications as are essentially requisite to be found in the persons that must partake of these substantial signs of the new covenant.

As for circumcision, it was not necessary for all that were circumcised to believe and repent, or to have faith in Christ, or to be converted and made disciples by preaching, as necessary qualifications to partake of the ordinances. But the institution in Genesis 17:13 saith, "He that is born in thy house, and he that is bought with thy money." Though never so ignorant, carnal, or have never so wicked parents or parentage, yet such ought to be circumcised, this institution running upon that family.

But baptism is a confirmation of our regeneration already wrought in us, and our new birth, and our union with Jesus Christ by faith, and therefore belongs only to them where this regeneration is, to them that are born again of water and of the Spirit. And so, the Passover was to be partaken of by the carnal Israelite after the flesh, namely, the captive, the slave bought with money, heathen, black moor, or of the Canaanites. But the Lord's supper only belongs to disciples able to discern the Lord's body by faith, without the which they bring judgement upon themselves, and make themselves guilty of the body and blood of the Lord, except they are able to examine themselves. "But let a man examine himself, and so let him eat of that bread, and drink of that cup."[147]

So that which the apostle drives at in this chapter is this principally: that as temporal Israel, who were the church of God then privileged in that temporal covenant upon their falls and sins,

---

[147] [1 Cor. 11:28.]

117

were by God visited and corrected to shew to all the world that he would not countenance sin in them without sad reproof. So he concludes in this also, the gospel-church, professing the covenant of grace and enjoying the privileges thereof, they should not escape if they turn aside from God and sin against him without checks, reproofs, and sad admonitions from him. And here lies the scope, and the rather might such caution be given to gospel-churches, because they were in a covenant of grace only by a visible profession, and therefore may possibly receive the greater danger by sin if their profession should not be right and saving.

OBJECTION

But some may object that there were some precious saints then in the Old Testament. And do you think that they did not perform the ordinances with spiritual hearts?

ANSWER. No question such did, as it is said of Abel, "By faith he offered a more excellent sacrifice than Cain."[148]

Duties performed from faith with an eye to Christ were then acceptable, when so performed, though ceremoniously, and such duties relating merely to the covenant of works.

Only I would have you to observe that the carnal Israelite was, without faith, capable to perform every ceremonial law required by the old covenant, according to the express tenor thereof, as truly as the believer.

So, in no wise can it be said of the duties relating to the new covenant, either then or now, as repentance, spiritual prayer,

---

[148] [Heb. 11:4.]

118

thanksgiving, and divers other duties, perpetually at all times, and universal to all saints. I deny that the carnal Jews were capable of the true performance of these; I mean as to answer the rules or institutions given. For if you look to the catechism in the Common Prayer Book, you shall find that it was a maxim received by all that own that liturgy, that no less than a profession of faith and repentance was required of them that were baptized.

Whence observe, they thereby confirm the doctrine that I have been all this while pleading for, that none but such as have faith and repentance in their hearts, and do profess the same, should be baptized.

OBJECTION

But may some say, "Did not some bring their friends to Christ to be healed, and Christ, seeing the faith of those which brought them, healed them? And if they believed for others, to the healing of their bodies, why not also then for the saving of their souls?"

ANSWER. This is directly the Papists argument with which some do close, rather than part with their idol. But to speak to this more particularly, there is nothing more plain than that God did give gifts of healing to many, as that the faith of one contributed to the healing of the body of another, as their servants and children, as in the case of the centurion in Matthew 8:7–9, and Jairus, the ruler over the synagogue.[149] But this is no way to prove that one man should come to have union with Christ and so to have justification and eternal life by the faith of another.

---

[149] [Mark 5:21–43; Luke 8:40–56.]

For in this case, the prophet saith, "The just shall live by his faith."[150] And he that believes not is condemned already,[151] that is, every individual that believes not shall be condemned, and he that believeth shall be saved. But some do bring in that text in the 7th of the Hebrews, that Levi paid tithes in Abraham, therefore why should not souls believe and repent in their believing parents, as well as Levi paid tithes in his believing father Abraham?

It seems to me that this act of Abraham was performed as a public person, in his paying tithes to Melchizedek, herein representing his posterity, but not so in all the rest of his acts. It doth not follow that he believed and repented for all his posterity, for this were a notable ground indeed for Papists' implicit faith.

We know that Adam, in his fall, did act sin as a public person, in which all mankind are said to sin.[152] But it doth not follow that all the future acts that Adam committed he did perform as a public person. For if all the posterity of a believing person, so many generations to come, as Levi from Abraham, did believe and repent in their believing parents, then there is no ground to oppose that all the world at this day are believers, because they were all in the line of believing Noah, he being the father from whence all the world did proceed that are now living this day.

And again, observe, that if the covenant of life belongs to all believers' seed, then we need not want for church members, because all the world are the children and offspring of believing Noah, and this argument carries the right of covenant to all the world, being the children of a believer, namely, Noah.

---

[150] Hab. 2:4; Rom. 1:17.

[151] [John 3:18.]

[152] Rom. 5.

MATTHEW 19:13–15

Further, some bring in Matthew 19:13–15.

> Then were there brought unto him little children, that he should put his hands on them, and pray: and the disciples rebuked them. But Jesus said, Suffer little children, and forbid them not, to come unto me: for of such is the kingdom of heaven. And he laid his hands on them, and departed thence.

In Mark 10:13–15, thus,

> And they brought young children to him, that he should touch them: and his disciples rebuked those that brought them. But when Jesus saw it, he was much displeased, and said unto them, Suffer the little children to come unto me, and forbid them not: for of such is the kingdom of God. Verily I say unto you, Whosoever shall not receive the kingdom of God as a little child, he shall not enter therein.

From hence would some maintain a covenant of eternal life in the flesh. For that end they bring this text, but let us examine what the meaning of it may be.

First, whose children they were that were brought to Christ doth not appear. It is probable they were the seed of Abraham, but what their mediate parents, whether believers or wicked persons, doth not appear certainly, but by the former discourse in the chapter it should seem they might be wicked and ungodly persons, for there were such mentioned before that tempted Christ and asked him questions.

The next thing is, for what did they bring these children unto

Christ? Most certainly not to baptize them, because Christ is said [to have] baptized not, but the disciples.[153] What then were they brought to Christ for? One Evangelist saith, "He took them in his arms and blessed them."[154] Another saith, "He laid his hands on them and prayed."[155]

All which considered, in my judgement, it doth probably appear they were brought to him to be healed of some disease, it being usual in those days that by prayer and laying on of hands they did heal the sick.

But the main expression in the text to be noted is this, "that of such are the kingdom of God." From these words, some gather that all the children of believing parents do belong to the kingdom of God, and if to the kingdom of God, then to all the privileges of that kingdom.

But, as you have heard, it will be very doubtful whether these children had any believing parents to the fifth or sixth degree, for of such is the kingdom of God, saith the text. The which we must understand thus: that all the children born of the body of believers, and that when little ones in arms do belong to the kingdom of God, if you will make this text to countenance that error of the covenant in the flesh, the which is erroneous as appears in that the greatest number of believers' children never belonged in that sense to the kingdom of God, for Adam had a Cain as well as an Abel; Noah had a Ham as well as a Shem; Abraham had an Ishmael as well as an Isaac; Isaac had an Esau as well as a Jacob. And so, I might mention all the Scriptures wherein, in like manner,

---

[153] John 4:2.

[154] [Mark 10:16.]

[155] [Matt. 19:13.]

122

God doth as well bring forth the generation of the wicked out of the godly, and the generation of the elect out of the line of the wicked indefinitely.

But if by kingdom of God be meant that condition or state that men are interested in by virtue of a covenant of eternal life, and that believers' children should, by birth and generation, belong to it, then this fully crosseth that doctrine of Christ to Nicodemus, as was formerly spoken to.[156]

OBJECTION

But some may say it is possible that such a little child may believe, because in Matthew 18:3–6 it is said we should not offend such little ones that believe.

ANSWER. If you grant that some children, when little, do believe, and therefore belong to the kingdom of God, to that I assent; let them be whose children they will, whether of believers or infidels. If they believe, they are in Christ, and so interested in the kingdom of God. But what makes this for the covenant in the flesh of carnal unbelieving seed?

Again, if by kingdom of God should be understood the Jewish state or church, and children here understood for children of that Jewish nation, then in that sense it is true that all the children born in the Jewish church, by virtue of their birth in that family or nation, belonged as members to that national church, being interested in the covenant of circumcision, which was the national covenant, and the privileges of the same, and were by natural

---

[156] John 3:5.

birth interested therein.

But the true and proper meaning of the text appears plain to be here in Mark 10:13–15 compared together, for when he had, in the 14th verse, said, "Of such belongeth the kingdom of God." In the 15th verse, he presently saith, "Verily I say unto you, whosoever receiveth not the kingdom of God, as a little child, shall not enter therein." This, I say, interprets these words before, "Of such as the kingdom of God," that is, of such like in grace as these be by nature, such souls that are by God's grace subdued and brought into a childlike frame of spirit, they only are such as are of the kingdom of God, as for example.

When the disciples reasoned who should be greatest among them, Christ set a little child as a pattern of humility, innocency, and harmlessness.[157]

And also, saith the apostle, "Howbeit in malice be ye children, but in understanding be men."[158] And saith Peter, "As newborn babes, desire the sincere milk of the word, that ye may grow thereby."[159]

And so, as there is a parity held forth between a man and his wife, and Christ and his church, so in Scripture there is between a child in nature and a child in grace, as the natural begetting, the spiritual begetting, alluding to that there is the natural birth and the spiritual birth held forth by that sucking of the mother's breast, and by sucking of the breast of God's word.

A little babe, we know in nature, will trust to his parents; so the newborn babe will trust in Christ. If the natural babe want

---

[157] [Luke 9:46–47.]

[158] 1 Cor. 14:20.

[159] 1 Pet. 2:2.

124

anything, it will go to its parents and ask them for it; so must a newborn babe make his request known to God in all his wants. If anything hurt a babe, he will cry, and make his complaint to his father; so the child of God. If any straight oppresseth him, he cries to God, his Father. The natural child will imitate his father and his brethren; so the newborn babe imitates God the Father and Christ, and the rest, as it were, of his brethren. The newborn babe, when young, a little will content it; so should the newborn babe in grace be in all conditions and states content.

And this, I understand, to be the proper meaning of this place, "Of such is the kingdom of God," that is, of such souls that are spiritually qualified by God's grace, answerable to little children in nature. Of such godly newborn heavenly babes is the kingdom of God.[160]

And this exposition agrees with the right scope of the place and the true analogy of faith.

And therefore, I would have you seriously to consider that this covenant of grace in the flesh, the whole word of the Lord disclaims it, and will give no countenance to any such notion so destructive in its consequence to the truth of God, as you have heard before.

OBJECTION

But some may object and say, "But this which you call a covenant of works, consisting of temporal promises, and also laws and statutes, you are not to understand that to be a distinct covenant from the covenant of eternal life, but a form of administration that the cov-

---

[160] Matt. 18:1–6.

enant of grace was then administered in. And the carnal children were not then interested in the main privileges of the covenant, as adoption and justification, but the outward promises and privileges only made to their fathers."

ANSWER. I know this objection some do bring, which if it be well weighed is inconsistent with their own arguments.

For if this objection be true, then was there no covenant made to Abraham's seed, but only an administration of a covenant. And therefore, ill do they affirm that the covenant was made to them, therefore the administration. But this doubtless is false, and this objection, as I said, is false and groundless, as appears by several express testimonies in Scripture which doth evidently prove two distinct covenants, as for example.

Saith God in Genesis 17:7, "And I will establish my covenant between me and thee and thy seed after thee in their generations for an everlasting covenant, to be a God unto thee, and to thy seed after thee." Where observe, that the Lord doth not say that he will establish an administration of the covenant with his seed in their generations, but his covenant, and Abraham and his seed, must keep his covenant. And in verse 13, "And my covenant shall be in your flesh for an everlasting covenant." Not, this administration of my covenant shall be in your flesh. And so, in Hebrews 8:6–9, "But now hath he obtained a more excellent ministry, by how much also he is the mediator of a better covenant, which was established upon better promises."

Mark, as I have before shewed at large, here were two covenants—the one upon better promises, the other upon worse promises, which must needs be understood temporal blessings, and deliverances, and privileges. Therefore, he saith they serve unto the example and shadow of heavenly things. And in Hebrews 8:7, "For if that first covenant had been faultless, then should no place have been sought for the second." And in 8:9 he saith that the old covenant they continued not in, therefore God regarded them not. And in 8:13 he saith, "A new *covenant*, he hath made the first old. Now that which decayeth and waketh old is ready to vanish away."

Which Scriptures do evidence, as clear as the sun at noon day, that there was a real covenant made with the Jews, made before with Abraham, but committed to the church in writing by Moses when he led them out of Egypt. And this covenant they brake, said Jeremiah 31:32. And here, the apostle saith they continued not in it, and the last verse saith it was made old, and therefore vanishing away. And in Hebrews 9, there the apostle calls this "old covenant," that contained in it shadows and patterns of heavenly things—the first testament, wherein the apostle in verse 17 and forwards doth shew there were two testaments, the one confirmed by the blood of bulls, the other confirmed by the blood of Christ. And if this were not true then, most falsely do such affirm, the covenant was made with Abraham's seed. Therefore the privileges, if Abraham lineally had no covenant made with them, [are] but only an external and outward administration and privilege, etc.

Upon that ground there was no national covenant at all made with Israel, but only an outward administration, and that being granted to be ceremonial, except you can prove another ceremonial administration as carnal as that administration was now in force. There is not the like ground why carnal and unbelieving children should have any share in it.

3

An Exposition of
Galatians 4:21–31

ut that there were two covenants is most evident, as appears in the New Testament, as I have formerly at large endeavoured to make good. Only, I shall add that in Galatians 4:21 and forward, where saith the apostle,

> Tell me, ye that desire to be under the law, do ye not hear the law? For it is written, that Abraham had two sons, the one by a bondmaid, the other by a freewoman. But he who was of the bondwoman was born after the flesh; but he of the freewoman was by promise. Which things are an allegory.

That is, by these things other things are meant.

> For these are the two covenants; the one from the mount Sinai, which gendereth to bondage, which is Agar. For this Agar is mount Sinai in Arabia, and answereth to Jerusalem which now is, and is in bondage with her children. But Jerusalem which is above is free, which is the mother of us all…. Now we, brethren, as Isaac was, are

the children of promise. But as then he that was born after the flesh persecuted him that was born after the Spirit, even so it is now. Nevertheless what saith the scripture? Cast out the bondwoman and her son: for the son of the bondwoman shall not be heir with the son of the freewoman. So then, brethren, we are not children of the bondwoman, but of the free.[1]

And in the next chapter he saith, "Stand fast therefore in the liberty wherewith Christ hath made us free, and be not entangled again with the yoke of bondage," which he afterwards explains to be the covenant of circumcision.[2]

But to speak something to this text, Abraham, here by the apostle, is understood to represent God by way of type and figure, as it were. His two women, Sarah and Hagar, the two covenants of God; the two sons, Ishmael and Isaac, represents, as the text hints, the two seeds in these two covenants of God. Now Sarah, the freewoman, represents the covenant of grace, and Hagar the covenant of works. Both these women continued in Abraham's house together for a time.

The first child he begat by the strength of nature, without faith in a promise, of a bondwoman. The other he begat by faith, in a promise without strength of nature, of a freewoman. And the freewoman continued in Abraham's house with the bondwoman and her son without any scruple till Isaac was born and also weaned. And when the son of the bondwoman persecuted Isaac, the freewoman testifies against the bondwoman and her

---

[1] [Gal. 4:24–31.]
[2] Gal. 5:1–3.

son, and will have them no longer to abide in the house with her son. Abraham, likewise, had first the freewoman and the last the bondwoman. The freewoman was sometime barren in Abraham's house, but the bondwoman was fruitful.

Now the mystery that the apostle hints to be held forth in this history is clear, from which he speaks in this 4th of the Galatians, which must be this.

That God, in like manner, first made a covenant of grace, even as Abraham first had a freewoman, which covenant, in a great measure, was barren, bringing forth no seed, or else totally barren as Sarah was, in respect of that substantial seed Christ Jesus, which Isaac typed forth as soon as God had made this covenant. He, in the same house or church, hath also a Hagar—that is, a covenant of works in which God hath abundance of seed becoming his by strength of nature, without faith in a promise and the covenant of grace, as Sarah, in a sense, becomes barren. All which time the covenant of grace and covenant of works both agree very well to be in God's house together.

But at the last, as the freewoman brought forth Isaac, so the covenant of grace brings forth Christ Jesus without strength of nature, by faith in a promise, as in Matthew 1:21 and Luke 1:35. And when this substantial seed is come, then the covenant of grace and works remain in God's church together. But afterwards, when Christ, the true Isaac, was, as it were, weaned—that is, come to maturity so as to appear that he was now in the office of the ministry—the scribes and Pharisees with the high priests, all the sons of Hagar, the old covenant, persecuted Christ and those in him.

Whereupon the freewoman, or rather the free covenant of grace, doth testify that a covenant of works with her seed shall no longer remain with her in the church of God.

But now, the free covenant and her sons, that is, the covenant of grace only and her children born by faith in a promise, only must for a time forward remain in the house of God.

So that now, rejoice thou barren that barest not, the covenant of grace becomes fruitful, having seed in all nations. Therefore, the apostle saith, "But Jerusalem which is above is free, which is the mother of us all."[3] And those [of] us, or we that were members of the primitive church, were born from above by faith in a promise.

Therefore, it is plain from hence that there were no carnal babes in that church. But when Christ, the true seed of the covenant, was persecuted by the Jews, which were the children of the covenant of works, the gospel doth plentifully testify the abolishing the covenant of works, and the casting forth of those bond-children out of God's church.

> But when the Jews saw the multitudes, they were filled with envy, and spake against those things which were spoken by Paul, contradicting and blaspheming. Then Paul and Barnabas waxed bold, and said, It was necessary that the word of God should first have been spoken to you: but seeing ye put it from you, and judge yourselves unworthy of everlasting life, lo, we turn to the Gentiles. For so hath the Lord commanded us.[4]

---

[3] [Gal. 4:26.]
[4] Acts 13:45–47.

And as appears in the 11th chapter of the Romans, and as that 4th chapter of Galatians in express words saith in the 25th verse, this Hagar is meant mount Sinai in Arabia, "and answereth to Jerusalem which now is, and is in bondage with her children." This being so clear, that the bondwoman and her son, that is, to say the covenant of works and all those related to Abraham, only in a covenant of works are cast out of the house of God.

How opposite then is their opinion to the truth that still would have a fleshly generation to be in the house of God with their children. But seeing the natural branches that truly were descended of the line of faithful Abraham might not have that honor, how much less the unbelieving seed of the Gentiles that are wild by nature?

Thus, you see in brief this objection answered, and that there is no ground for children's baptism, but an imagination through thick darkness, upon the minds of people—they, setting up this idol in their hearts. God hath answered them accordingly, as the prophet speaks in Ezekiel 14:2–5,

> And the word of the LORD came unto me, saying, Son of man, these men have set up their idols in their heart, and put the stumblingblock of their iniquity before their face: should I be enquired of at all by them? Therefore speak unto them, and say unto them, Thus saith the Lord GOD; Every man of the house of Israel that setteth up his idols in his heart, and putteth the stumblingblock of his iniquity before his face, and cometh to the prophet; I the LORD will answer him that cometh according to the multitude of his idols; That I may take the house of Israel

in their own heart, because they are all estranged from me through their idols.

Where you see, that when souls set up an idol in their heart, God doth answer them according to their idol, as he hath in this case, suffering blind blindness and uncertainty of judgment to befall them.

For such as defend children's baptism, and the ablest I have met with, do grant they have no command or example in the New Testament for their practice, but ground the same on a consequence, which you have heard evidently proved is drawn from an error. For to affirm or maintain that the covenant of eternal life is made with believers' carnal seed is a dangerous error, and therefore the consequence must needs be as false and rotten as that error from whence it is drawn, then judge you what a pitiful consequence that must be.

Take the whole result thus, children's baptism hath no ground from the word of God, either command or example for it, but a consequence, as before, so that it is merely a tradition of men set up in the place and room of the commands of God, to wit, baptizing of believers. This groundless tradition makes void the commandment of God, even as the wicked Jews did in Mark 7:7, "Howbeit in vain do they worship me, teaching for doctrines the commandments of men." And in verse 9, "And he said unto them, Full well ye reject the commandment of God, that ye may keep your own tradition." And in verse 13, "Making the word of God of none effect through your tradition, which ye have delivered: and many such like things do ye."

Now, beloved, this is the very sin of such as defend this tradition: they thereby make void and frustrate the commandment of God, where Christ saith, "Repent, and be baptized every one of you,"[5] that is, every one that repents. And saith Ananias to Paul, "Arise, and be baptized, and wash away thy sins, calling on the name of the Lord." [6]And Peter to Cornelius [and] his family, he there commands them to be baptized in the name of the Lord Jesus.[7] Those, and many more standing commands of the New Testament, that belong to believers and penitent persons are frustrated and made void by christening children.

Thus, poor souls are nursed up in a habit of disrespect and disobedience to these commandments because this invention takes the place and room of the same.

Do but consider how dangerous a sin this practice is; it is setting up a superstitious invention in the room of God's command in his worship.

Now God and his commandments must not be separated, for a soul that rightly sets up God's commandments sets up and exalts God, and to set up any worship in the room of what is commanded of God is, in effect, to set up a false God.

Do but see what sad witnesses God hath given from heaven against this sin in Leviticus 10:1–2, where Nadab and Abihu offered strange fire to God, as the text saith, which he commanded not, for which God burned them with fire from heaven. The Lord doth not say which he had *forbidden*, but which he *commanded not*. Many souls ask where God hath forbid this practice of children's baptism. Therefore, I would prove by these Scriptures that

---

[5] [Acts 2:38.]

[6] [Acts 22:16.]

[7] Acts 10:48.

things or persons in the worship of God, in room of what God commands, are abominable to God. Hear how God doth threaten a people for this sin in Jeremiah 9:13–15, "And the LORD saith, Because they have forsaken my law which I set before them, and have not obeyed my voice, neither walked therein; But have walked after the imagination of their own heart." Therefore, he saith in verse 15, "I will feed them, even this people, with wormwood, and give them water of gall to drink."

Now this is the very case of such as set up this tradition. They forsake the law of believer's baptism set before them, and have never obeyed his voice, nor walked therein, but have walked in children's sprinkling, which the imagination of their own hearts have devised. This text is very much applicable to such souls; the like evil wicked Saul is said to do, for which God rends the kingdom from him,[8] and in Jeremiah 8:9–10, "The wise men are ashamed, they are dismayed and taken: lo, they have rejected the word of the LORD; and what wisdom is in them? Therefore will I give their wives unto others, and their fields to them that shall inherit them." And so, in Jeremiah 7:31, "They have built the high places of Tophet, which is in the valley of the son of Hinnom, to burn their sons and their daughters in the fire; which I commanded them not, neither came it into my heart," upon which he threatens destruction upon them.

And you see how God made a breach upon Uzzah for touching the ark, God not commanding him or giving him rule for such practice, God having given a command to the priests only to do that work, but not to him. So God hath given a command

---

[8] 1 Sam. 13:12–13.

and example to baptize believers only, and not children. There-fore, it is the sin of Uzzah, and likewise the sin of King Uzziah, where you see the sad judgement of God upon Uzziah for doing that in the worship of God which God had not commanded in the room or stead of what he had commanded.[9] God struct him with leprosy, and that in his forehead, and the hand of God pros-ecuted him as an admonition to persons that now dare adventure upon the like sinful practices, to offer anything to God as reli-gious worship which he hath not commanded, instead of what he hath commanded.

The Lord, in this case, sets out himself to be a jealous God that will visit the sins of the father upon the children to the third and fourth generation, of such as make to themselves any graven image, that is, any form by which we will worship God. Be sure it is of God's own making, for we must not make it to ourselves. The Lord doth call in Scripture such like worship which men do in the room of God's commanded worship, "the worship of dev-ils." I shall give you one instance for this in Scripture, as in Psalm 106:35–36, "And they served their idols: which were a snare unto them. Yea, they sacrificed their sons and their daughters unto devils." And the next verse, expounding himself, it is said, "they sacrificed unto the idols of Canaan." And in like manner, do not men bring their sons and their daughters, in this case, and offer them to this invention of sprinkling?

You have for baptizing of believers the commandment of Christ, and testimony of the infallible penmen, and all men in the world owning the Scriptures to be the word of God, to be of

---

[9] 2 Chr. 26:14–15.

the Lord's own institution. But this practice of children's sprin-kling, God hath raised up in all ages some that have professed religion to witness against it, and a great part of those that have the power of godliness do renounce it as a sinful practice, and that upon substantial grounds. And methinks when you consider that your children's sprinkling hath no command or example in the gospel to confirm it, and only such a consequence, that flows from an error.

I hope such as fear God will take heed how they harden their hearts in the practice of so heinous a sin, and in the neglect of so solemn a duty as the ordinance of dipping believers in the name of the Father, Son and Holy Ghost. For is there any man able to declare from Scripture that ever any solemn ordinance of stand-ing use in the church of the New Testament had, for its institu-tion, any less than a command of God and a promise of blessing to the faithful performance of the same? But there is for children's baptism neither command to institute, nor any promise to bless, but rather indeed the performers of that worship may expect a curse, and not a blessing, in the performance of the same, as you have it in Psalm 99:8, "Thou answeredst them, O LORD our God: thou wast a God that forgavest them, though thou tookest vengeance of their inventions." With Psalm 106:29, "Thus they provoked him to anger with their inventions: and the plague brake in upon them," as it did in the 2 Chronicles 26:19–21,

> Then Uzziah was wroth, and had a censer in his hand to burn incense: and while he was wroth with the priests, the leprosy even rose up in his forehead before the priests in the house of the LORD, from beside the incense altar.

And Azariah the chief priest, and all the priests, looked upon him, and, behold, he was leprous in his forehead, and they thrust him out from thence; yea, himself hasted also to go out, because the LORD had smitten him. And Uzziah the king was a leper unto the day of his death, and dwelt in a several house, being a leper; for he was cut off from the house of the LORD.

Thus, you see the sad curse of God executed against such like inventions in the service of God that men set up in the room of God's commands, thereby justling out his commands, as the Scripture saith.

This is for a man to set up his posts by God's posts, and in a sense, setting up himself in the place and room of God, and flows from abundance of pride, as here it is said of King Uzziah, preceding this, his sin [and] his heart was lifted up to his own destruction.

Now most certain it is that [that] man Moses was faithful in all God's house, as a servant, in giving the church then exact and perfect rules—how they should serve God, unto which they must not add, and from which they must not detract nor take away.[10] So Christ is every way as faithful over his house as a Lord,[11] and rightly to this purpose is applied that in Colossians 2:8 with 2:20–22.

For men to embrace any worship to their God that they have not a rule for, it is in that chapter condemned as will-worship and traditions of men. And warily consider that it fosters men

---

[10] Deut. 4:2.
[11] Heb. 3:4–6.

in a sinful neglect of that holy and solemn ordinance of dipping believers.

Do not all our Protestant authors, in all their disputations against the Papists, defend that faith and repentance precede baptism, thereby confuting the Papists that baptism is not to convey grace where it is not, but to confirm grace, and strengthen it where it is?

And in that catechism embraced generally by all Protestants in the common liturgy in England, this question is demanded, "What is required of them that are to be baptized?" The answer is "faith and repentance," which doth plainly manifest that it was the judgement of all those that were Protestants owning that liturgy, that none ought to be baptized, but such as repent and believe. Not only so, but that do confess faith and repentance, because in baptism there is, as Peter saith, "The answer of a good conscience."[12] Compared with Philip and the eunuch, "If thou believest with all thine heart, thou mayest." Saith the eunuch, "I believe that Jesus Christ is the Son of God."[13] So in Acts 19:18 it is said, "And many that believed came, and confessed, and shewed their deeds."

Now consider that this doctrine, in all those times, was defended that faith and repentance must needs precede baptism. Why? Because they concluded it a seal of the new covenant, and therefore where persons were not in a covenant by faith, did in opposition to the Papists defend, they had no interest in baptism.

Now let any soul that is not blinded with the subtilty of Satan,

---

[12] 1 Pet. 3:19.

[13] Acts 8:37.

and by means of the stumbling block of iniquity set up in his own heart, as saith the Lord in Ezekiel 14:4, let such, I say, judge how cross to this doctrine they do practice that do baptize visible, graceless, and Christless children, so far as any man is able to judge.

4

Baptism and the Visible Church

But some will say, "I grant this, [that the] baptizing of children is a mere tradition and that not to be practised by Christians, and I do believe in the primitive time believers only had this ordinance dispenesd upon them. But I do conceive, saith the soul, I have received the baptism of the Holy Ghost, therefore I need not that ordinance of baptism by water, and the rather, because I think that was John's baptism, and the baptism of the Holy Ghost being come hath put an end to that baptism of water."

NSWER. Then you deny in judgement any ordinance of baptism at all to stand in force, which is, be sure, an upstart opinion, exceedingly cross to the doctrine of Christ in his gospel. But let me, as warily as I can, answer this question.

First, you do think it was John's baptism. It is true that John baptized, or dipped into water, those that came to him confessing their sins, and professing faith in him that should come after him.

But though it is true [that] John's baptism, in this respect, pointing out Christ to come is done away, yet it is as true that the

142

Lord hath afresh, since his death and resurrection, instituted this ordinance of dipping believers into Christ already come and fully exhibited in the flesh.[1] The Holy Ghost was, in that extraordinary manner, powered down upon him according to John's prophesy, to wit, with cloven fiery tongues. He doth, after this, by the direction of the infallible Spirit, command all his converts that were pricked in the heart to repent and be baptized every one of them for the remission of sins, and they should receive the gift of the Holy Ghost.[2]

Where you may see that this was [a] baptism of water that he commanded all that repent to submit to, because the Holy Ghost, as those extraordinary gifts was to follow, to wit, those gifts that Joel prophesied of. And so, in Acts 10, when Cornelius and his house had heard the word of God, the Holy Ghost fell upon them, and as an effect thereof they spake with new tongues and magnified God. And then saith Peter to them of the circumcision, "Can any man forbid water, that these should not be baptized, which have received the Holy Ghost as well as we?" So that this great apostle was so far from this opinion that he urgeth the contrary, that because they had received the Holy Ghost, and that in the extraordinary gifts thereof, which John foretold Christ should baptize them with, saith he, "How shall we forbid water," plainly holding forth that it is baptism by water that he here is speaking of, and in which verse 48 he commanded them to be baptized in the name of the Lord Jesus because they received the Holy Ghost.

Therefore, they must not be denied that ordinance of baptism

---

[1] Matthew 28:19–20; Mark 16:16; and Peter. [Patient likely is referencing 1 Pet. 3:21.]

[2] Acts 2:38.

by water, clearly holding forth that the enjoying the Holy Ghost was so far from being an argument why souls should not be baptized with water that it is an argument that they ought to be baptized more especially.

And this appears in Paul after his conversion, which I understand was wrought by Christ immediately. For saith he to Ananias, "For he is a chosen vessel unto me."[3] Therefore, say I, he was now converted as to the inward work of faith, changing his heart. But when Ananias came to him, he laid his hands upon him, and there were two effects of this, his laying on of his hands—he received his sight and was filled with the Holy Ghost, and he arose forthwith and was baptized.[4] That is to say, after he was filled with the Holy Ghost, he arose and was baptized in water.[5] When Paul had received the Holy Ghost, Ananias saith, "And now why tarriest thou? arise, and be baptized, and wash away thy sins, calling on the name of the Lord."[6]

Observe that Ananias had an immediately extraordinary commission from Christ, by vision, to come with the message to Paul. And Christ, in a vision, bids Paul go to Ananias, and he should tell him what he should do. And Ananias, according to that commission of Christ, upon his being filled with the Holy Ghost, commands him to be baptized. And this agrees with the covenant of grace in Ezekiel 36:27, where the Lord saith, "And I will put my spirit within you, and cause you to walk in my statutes." And Ezekiel 11:19–20,

---

[3] [Acts 9:15.]
[4] [Acts 9:17–18.]
[5] Acts 9:17–18 compared with Acts 22:16.
[6] [Acts 22:16.]

> And I will give them one heart, and I will put a new spirit
> within you; and I will take the stony heart out of their
> flesh, and will give them an heart of flesh: That they may
> walk in my statutes, and keep mine ordinances, and do
> them: and they shall be my people, and I will be their
> God.

Where you may see that God is so far from giving his Spirit
to the end that souls should plead, thereby, freedom from the
practice of those commanded ordinances of Christ; that on the
contrary, it is the end why God gives his Spirit, to enable and
to cause them to walk in his way, and in his ordinances, and in
particular baptism.

And observe, the apostles have not left us a bare example—
only that they did baptize after Christ powered out the Holy
Ghost, and that by the authority received from heaven—but doth
command it, as you have heard to all that repent and believe, and
to all that receive the Holy Ghost to submit to it.

But again, the baptism of the Holy Ghost and fire that John
foretold of, it is clear, was extraordinarily given upon an especial ground and reason fulfilled in Acts 2. The Holy Ghost falling
down in fiery cloven tongues in the sight and view of the bodily
eyes, which was that outward sign, and that clear light, and fervent zeal, and love they had, in uttering the wonderful things of
God in variety of strange tongues, was the inward thing signified,
so that herein the baptism of the Holy Ghost was an outward
sign, and an inward thing signified. But there is now no man in
the world [that] hath this baptism. Only, it is true, that the Spirit,
in the saving gifts of faith, repentance, and the like, is held to

be essential to the ordinance of baptism of water, and must be joined together with it, without which it cannot be said to be an ordinance of God. There must be the inward grace, as well as the outward sign.

This baptism that the apostle, according to Christ's commission, hath left a standing command for cannot be John's baptism, his holding forth Christ to come, baptizing them in that doctrine. But in this we baptize persons in—Christ already come and fully exhibited.

And though it may be objected that the apostles practiced some things that were abolished, as the circumcising of Timothy and the like, we also say that as they practised it among the Jews, so the apostle Paul to the Gentiles saith, if they be circumcised Christ should profit them nothing, but they were fallen from grace.[7] And we never find that circumcision was practised among the Gentiles that were void of all religion before they taught them.

It is evident in the New Testament that circumcision is abolished as part of the mosaical covenant, and yoke of bondage.[8] But the case in baptism is clean otherwise.

Whereas you hear, the apostle did press Cornelius [and] his family to be baptized, who was a Gentile never acquainted with John's baptism, nor wedded to such a doctrine as that whereby we should think that Peter did baptize them to condescended to that error or weakness in their minds.

Again, he doth not only simply baptize them as a liberty that might be done or not done, but commands them to be baptized,

---

[7] [Gal. 5:2.]
[8] Gal. 5:1–3.

and so doth, as you heard before he did, in Acts 2. And it cannot be said that the apostles commanded any duty to be done with a promise of blessing to the right performance of the same after the Holy Ghost came down upon them, but it must needs be a solemn standing ordinance of God, that every soul upon pain of the guilt and rebellion against Christ, his head and king, ought to be subject unto.

But this of baptism, hath as aforesaid, many standing laws left in holy record, speaking to all that believe and repent, promising remission of sins and salvation to the right performance of the same, which proves it to be a standing ordinance of the New Testament.

And truly with the same reason souls may affirm that Christ ceaseth to be a mediator, as to hold the law of dipping believers ceaseth, so much and no less is affirmed by the soul that saith the ordinance of baptism is an expired ordinance. He may as well say Christ is expired and abolished as a fleshly form, as some have had the confidence to say.

For as in the time of Moses' ministration till there was a change of the priesthood, there could not be a change of the law. No more now, except there be another Christ and Saviour come, or another priesthood instead of this priest and minister of the New Testament. Assure yourselves, there can be no change of this law, as in Hebrews 7:12, 18.

Therefore, such as pretend to profess Christ to be their Saviour, that came of the seed of David, and the same persons deny and slight this fundamental ordinance of baptism, they do therein testify that they reject Christ in their heart as abolished, and have got some pretended fancy Christ instead of him. It is utterly inconsistent with the faith of the gospel, and with true religion, to hold baptism and the supper [as] two solemn ordinances and symbols of the new covenant to be abolished. For in Ephesians 4, the apostle, pressing there a visible church-union, lays down the main things wherein that union consists, called, saith he, by [the] one hope of their calling, one Spirit, one Lord, one faith, one baptism.[9] This one baptism cannot be meant the Spirit, because the Spirit is mentioned distinct. But baptism here must needs be meant that standing solemn ordinance of God commanded to everyone that believes.

Now the apostle, pressing here a church-union, doth mention these particulars that are essential to a visible church-union, without which they could not walk together, if not in these things agreed, and where a people in all these particulars are one, no other thing coming should make a breach of their union.

OBJECTION

But some other souls will object and say that believers baptism is an ordinance of God, and he thinks they do well that are drawn out to practice it, by a power from God. But, saith the soul, I want a divine power upon my heart, drawing me out to the practice of the same, and that is the let and hinderance in me.

ANSWER. This objection is grounded upon an error and a mistake, taking for granted that a man may be a believer, and in a state of grace, and yet void of spiritual power to perform obedi-

---

[9] [Eph. 4:4–5.]

ence to the commands of God, and that a man that is a Christian may know such a thing to be a command of God, and yet left without ability to perform obedience to the same.

I judge this is a dangerous error and contrary to Scripture. For God doth, at the very first conversion, put his law in the heart of his child.[10] God is said to put his Spirit in them to that end to cause them to walk in his ways, therefore in some measure, doubtless, God doth give his people power to obey him, as in Ezekiel 11:19–20,

> And I will give them one heart, and I will put a new spirit within you; and I will take the stony heart out of their flesh, and will give them an heart of flesh: That they may walk in my statutes, and keep mine ordinances, and do them: and they shall be my people, and I will be their God.

Whence you may observe, that God's main drift in making his covenant and giving his Spirit into the hearts of his people is that they may keep his ordinances, and be able to walk in his ways.

Therefore, at the first conversion of Paul, God puts in him a disposition to obedience. For saith he, "Lord, what wilt thou have me to do?"[11] In Acts 9, and so in Acts 2:37, when they, through the belief of Peter's sermon, were pricked at the heart, they cried out, "Men and brethren, what shall we do?" So you see, there was a disposition of heart, in their first conversion, to be doing what God should command and teach them to be his will. So we find God gives them power to submit as soon as his will was revealed,

---

[10] Heb. 8:10; Eze. 36:26–27
[11] [Acts 9:6.]

for if not so, we should lay an aspersion upon God that he should enter into a covenant with a soul by way of engagement, and yet neglect to make good his promise, which is to put his Spirit in him and to cause him to walk in his ways.

And again further, God gives to every believer the power of believing, by virtue of which he is enabled to fetch virtue from Christ, his head, to strengthen him to duty, and to resist sin. Therefore, the apostle thus reasons in 2 Corinthians 7:1, "Having therefore these promises, dearly beloved, let us cleanse ourselves from all filthiness of the flesh and spirit, perfecting holiness in the fear of God."

Whence observe, the apostle takes for granted the soul having great and precious promises, and faith to draw virtue from them, should thereby, oppose sin and perfect holiness in the fear of God. For though it is true God works to will and to do of his good pleasure, yet it is constantly and unfailingly his good pleasure, thus, to work more or less in a soul that is in him thus by faith. And a believer, by faith, ought to look at himself in a capacity to draw water out of those wells of salvation. For else, what difference [is there] between a child of God and a wicked man, the form of godliness and the power, if a child of God must be forced to live in a course of disobedience to the solemn worship of God for want of power to obey? And by the same rule we must take for granted that a child of God may be in a state of grace, and want power to resist sin, and upon this ground plead excuse for drunkenness, and covetousness, and theft or uncleanness, and say though he is a believer, yet he wants power to resist and conquer these sins.

Beloved, thus for any to plead would be very absurd and contrary to the truth, and the nature of a Christian in a state of grace. And further, observe the deceit lying in this objection.

Hath not God given thy soul power to hear the word of God, and to read, and to meditate, and to pray, and that sometimes earnestly and fervently to God? Is it likely that there wants power to perform obedience to this ordinance of baptism any more than thou doest perform prayer or other duties which require the same spiritual power upon due examination? What enabling power is required in the one more than in the other?

Again, consider, thou dost in this walk by sense, and not by faith, contrary to the apostle in 2 Corinthians 5:7, who saith, "We walk by faith, not by sight." It is a very childish thing in a Christian to walk by sense only. When he feels strength and power sensibly, then he thinks himself able to perform duty and resist sin, but when he feels not ability and power, then to neglect it. Whereas contrary to this, Christ saith to Paul in 2 Corinthians 12:9, "My grace is sufficient for thee: for my strength is made perfect in weakness." And as after, Paul expresseth himself, "When I am weak, then I am strong."[12]

When Paul was made most sensible of his own weakness in himself, then was the time for Paul to be made most strong by faith in the strength of another. Therefore, in Isaiah 45:24, "In the LORD have I righteousness and strength." In him shall they boast. And the psalmist saith in Psalm 73:26, "My flesh and my heart faileth: but God is the strength of my heart, and my portion for ever." So that when in a man's own sense his heart fails, his

---

[12] [2 Cor. 12:10.]

flesh fails. Then is the only time for God's strength to appear in his weakness. This is the way of living by faith, and the way which God's believing children have been carried.

Therefore, we find Jonah, when, in his own sense, he was cast out of God's sight, then he resolved to look towards God's holy temple, and cried to God out of the belly of hell.[13] Therefore, surely this objection hath no weight in it.

OBJECTION

But some other soul may say, "I grant the practice of baptism to be an ordinance of God, and the way of such churches that walk under the baptism of believers to be that only justifiable practice in the gospel, and could willingly walk with them and be baptized were it not for their rigidness in that they will have no communion with any, though godly, that are not baptized."

ANSWER. To this I answer by way of distinction between church-union and communion, and personal-union and communion. Now if we find a soul not baptized, nor joined to any church, and happily ignorant of baptism, yet if I have ground in my own heart to judge that soul to be godly, and not an enemy to the truth, and [the] gospel of Christ but a soul willing to hear and learn what truth God shall further reveal unto him, and so having ground to judge such a soul to have union and personal communion with the Lord, in such a case I ought to imitate the Lord in owning a communion with such a Christian, in like manner, as for example.

---

[13] Jon. 2.

Cornelius and his family, having a personal union with the Lord and communion with him before Peter preached to him, and he not being an obstinate professed enemy against any law of Christ, but contrarywise, saying to Peter, "We all here present before God, to hear all things that are commanded thee of God."[14]

Therefore, the Spirit of God falling down upon them, they spake with new tongues, and glorified God. And Peter and the six baptized brethren being with them, no question did join in Spirit and heart in that present spiritual service which Cornelius and his family did perform to God—they, none of them, at that interim of time being baptized, nor convinced that baptism was an ordinance of God. For till Peter had consulted with the brethren, he did not press baptism upon them. And therefore, we find that he did instruct them after a consultation which he had with the brethren, saying, "Can any man forbid water, that these should not be baptized, which have received the Holy Ghost as well as we?[15]

And Paul, in like manner, between the time that Christ had converted him and his coming to Ananias, prayed. And we find God owns a personal communion with him in that prayer. For Christ, speaking to Ananias, saith that Paul was a chosen vessel, "for, behold, he prayeth,"[16] manifesting that he owned Paul in that service.

Now, he being in a teachable godly frame, though ignorant of baptism, in prayer God had communion with him. In like manner, I judge from these Scripture examples, it is lawful for a bap-

---

[14] [Acts 10:33.]
[15] [Acts 10:47.]
[16] [Acts 9:11.]

tized person to have fellowship in prayer or speaking with any such soul which he is persuaded of to be godly, and that is not a professed enemy to any command of God.

But God hath not, as we find, ever had any church-union or communion with any soul that was unbaptized. And it is clear that the ordinance of the supper is committed to a church, yea to a ministerial assembly, gathered according to Christ's commission. [See] Matthew 28:19–20, where I understand the order there binding is this: First, the ministers should teach the nations, or make them disciples by teaching. And then the command is baptizing them. What "them?" Such that are made disciples by teaching. Thirdly, the command is to teach them to observe whatsoever Christ hath commanded. What "them" is here meant, but such as are made disciples and baptized, teaching them to observe whatsoever I have commanded you? "And I will be with you to the end of the world," that is, he will be with a people first converted, secondly baptized, thirdly walking in the practical observation of all other administrations of God's house, as these eleven did, and those they converted. I say, this, his promise, is to be with his people to the end of the world.

And this order is binding, that as a minister is commanded to baptize one, made a disciple, and not any other, so he is commanded to put them upon the practical observation of all his laws, and they only. And till they are baptized, they are not, nor cannot be, admitted into a visible church to partake of the supper of the Lord.

And that this is the true meaning of Christ in the commission appears by his apostles' ministry and practice, who by the infallible gifts of the Holy Ghost were guided unfailingly thus to preach and practice, as in Acts 2:37–38, 41–42. First, he teacheth them the doctrine of Jesus Christ. They hearing that were pricked at the heart, and inquiring of Peter, and the rest of the apostles, what they should do, he saith, "Repent, and be baptized every one of you." See how he presseth the same order here as Christ doth in the commission, and afterwards in the 41st verse it is said, "Then they that gladly received his word were baptized: and the same day there were added unto them about three thousand souls," by faith and baptism, "And they continued stedfastly in the apostles' doctrine and fellowship,   and in breaking of bread, and in prayers."[17]

Therefore, the way that Christ hath ordained is that souls should be joined or added to the church by faith and baptism, according to that word in 1 Corinthians 12:13, "For by one Spirit are we all baptized into one body."

Now though the Spirit, as the inward thing signified, be here spoken of, yet the outward sign is also included, as might be by other Scriptures cleared. Thus, Cornelius [and] his family were converted [and] then baptized before they were constituted a church.

So the jailors and Lydia's, and the church of Samaria in Acts 8, were all gathered by faith and dipping. And for a minister to gather a church any other way is to go not only in an untrodden path, but cross and point blank contrary to the doctrine and practice of the apostles, and thereby slight the rules of Christ in the commission, by which the apostles' doctrine and practice

---

[17] [Acts 2:41–42.]

was guided, and which all the ministers of the gospel ought to be guided by.

But yet further, the ordinance of baptism is to confirm our regeneration, new birth, and union with Christ in his death, burial, and resurrection.[18] And therefore, is to be received but once, as a man is to be regenerated but once, and born but once, and changed from death to life but once. But that ordinance of God, namely, the supper, is for Christian growth, and increase of grace, and of constant use, to shew forth Christ's death till he come, and therefore to be received often.

Now it must needs be a profanation of this ordinance of God to divert and cross the order, and so the special intendment of God in them, and that is, to admit persons to that ordinance which is principally for Christian growth before you have admitted them to that ordinance which is for planting them into Christ, signifying the confirmation or washing of regeneration, and the new birth and union with Christ, the true stock and root from whence all spiritual growth is to be expected.

Therefore, baptism must be the first ordinance dispensed or administered after conversion before the supper, so that it would be a profanation of the ordinances of God to divert their proper order, end, and use, to which our holy and jealous God hath appointed them. And it is a tender point for those that profess themselves friends to Christ, the bridegroom, to be venturing to take his peculiar privilege or prerogative out of his hands, as to order and dispose of his own order in his solemn worship, contrary to his commission.

---

[18] Rom. 6:3–5; Col. 2:12; Tit. 3:5.

I do judge such a man that hath not a tender conscience, in such cases, is in that much unlike Christ, and shews much carnality, because, as you have heard, God will have the honor to direct his people, both for the matter and manner of their worship, and order of his house.

But again, as you have heard before, in Ephesians 4:3–4 there is, by the apostle, mentioned these things that are essential to a particular visible church-union, which are these.

First, to be all called into the one hope of our calling,[19] which the poor children which some admit into their society by sprinkling are not called to the same hope that believers are called into. Again, one body, one Spirit, one faith, one Lord, and one baptism, one God and Father of us all.[20]

Now it is impossible that a people should walk together acceptably that have not one hope of one and the same glorious inheritance, and that have not one and the same Spirit and assistance and guidance in his holy worship, and that have not one and the same faith, but in the doctrine of faith do mainly differ one from another. And it is an essential difference, inconsistent with communion, that the members of one church should own two baptisms, the sprinkling of infants and dipping of believers. And this ordinance of baptism is one of the essentials of a true visible church.

And lastly, they are to own "one God and Father of all."[21] Here you have, from this text, a ground why such as are not enlightened in the Lord's baptism cannot be admitted into church fel-

---

[19] [Eph. 4:4.]
[20] [Eph. 4:4–6.]
[21] [Eph. 4:6.]

lowship, because in one and the same fellowship there is to be owned as one hope, one Spirit, one Lord, one faith, so one and the same baptism.

Again, the main end of church fellowship is that they there do practice whatsoever Christ hath commanded, as you have heard before in Matthew 28:20 and as Cornelius saith in Acts 10. "We all here present before God, to hear all things that are commanded thee of God."[22] And saith Christ, "Ye are my friends, if ye do whatsoever I command you."[23]

And this is, without doubt, that the true and lawful ministry in Christ's church is to see that all the members practice the observation of whatsoever he hath commanded, and so to see all the laws of Christ put in execution. For that cause hath Christ given into his church not only the key of doctrine, but also the key of discipline, that if any soul in a church shall be known, wittingly or willingly, to neglect any duty that the Lord hath commanded by his holy word, especially a fundamental ordinance of the New Testament, as is baptism and the supper of the Lord, it is without all question that such a soul, standing out in that disobedience, ought to be cast out of the church speedily for the same, without which the church, allowing or conniving at, or tolerating a soul in one course of known disobedience, do thereby make the sin their own, the whole people becoming really guilty of his sin and impiety. And as the apostle saith, thus will the whole lump be leavened, and that church unchurched.[24]

Amongst men, he that concealeth murder and is privy and

---

[22] [Acts 10:33.]
[23] [John 15:14.]
[24] [cf. 1 Cor. 5:6; Gal. 5:9.]

consenting to it, and will agree to tolerate it, is reckoned a murderer. In like manner, in the case of theft. Now the main end of church fellowship and ministerial power is to destroy sin, and to execute the power of Christ against it, and not to be fosterers and countenancers of sin, which you are if you agree to admit any person into your fellowship that refuseth to submit to baptism, that plain solemn ordinance of the New Testament; let his pretense be what it will be.

That person that is not brought over to yield obedience to whatsoever Christ hath commanded is not, while so disobedient, fit matter for a visible gospel-church, especially in those his fundamental ordinances as prayer, hearing, baptism and the supper of the Lord, thanksgiving, contribution to the necessity of the saints, and maintenance of an official ministry according to the ability that God gives them.

And by the same rule, and upon the same ground that you will tolerate some members in the church to live in the neglect of baptism, you must tolerate such as neglect to hear the word; and others that will not, according to ability, contribute to pious charitable uses; and others that will not pray in half a year or at twelve months together under the pretense they are not moved to that duty; and others that will in a gross manner neglect the duty of particular callings or relations, which the apostle in 2nd Thessalonians doth give rule to be withdrawn from, which is as the rest but the neglect of duty.[25] Nay, this practice lays a foundation for all disobedience, and for gathering an assembly of rebels; let me alone in my sin, and I will let thee alone in thine.

---

[25] [cf. 2 Thess. 3:10.]

OBJECTION

But may some say, "Is a godly mans omitting to be baptized or dipped a sin?"

ANSWER. Yes, certainly it is. For 1 John 3:4, the apostle saith sin is a transgression of the law.

Now you have heard several laws of the New Testament do command that such as believe and repent should be baptized. Therefore, to neglect is a transgression of those laws, and sincere obedience is universal obedience. By this, saith David, "Then shall I not be ashamed, when I have respect unto all thy commandments."[26]

But further consider, if you receive a person into communion that doth not submit to the Lord's baptism, that soul justifies still a corrupt baptism that he had in his infancy, and consequently is not ashamed of all he hath done amiss, which Ezekiel speaks of,[27] but still stands in fellowship and communion with a church and ministry which, by the bishop's power, dispensed the same. And you, receiving such a soul into communion, receive that church and ministry from which he had his supposed baptism, and must certainly own all those churches which that ministry stood in fellowship with that so baptized him. Therefore, it is a sad [somber] and serious matter who it is that is admitted into fellowship in the true church of Christ. And I would admonish souls to be careful that they do what they do in good order. For God it is said made a breach upon Uzzah because he did not do what he did in

---

[26] [Psa. 119:6.]
[27] [cf. Eze. 43:11.]

due order.

But some may say faith in Christ brings a soul into sonship, and so to a right in all the privileges in God's house.

ANSWER. It is true [that] faith and repentance doth entitle a soul, but repentance according to the gospel is a change of the heart, and a resolution to obey God in all his commandments. Such a repentance only the church of Christ ought to own in those members they receive. And therefore, though they ought to receive the weak in faith, yet they have no rule to receive them but by faith and baptism. So that though faith gives an interest to baptism, yet faith and baptism are to prepare and fit a soul for communion. "Then they that gladly received his word were baptized: and the same day there were added unto them about three thousand souls. And they continued stedfastly in the apostles' doctrine and fellowship, and in breaking of bread, and in prayers."[28]

So here you see the word of Christ our Lord, unto whom we ought to submit, that those only who were baptized were admitted into the fellowship of the saints and to breaking of bread, and therefore we, upon these grounds, may not admit any member in communion into the church of Christ but by baptism.

OBJECTION

But some may object and say, "There are many godly souls that do

---

[28] [Acts 2:41–42.]

think they are baptized already in their infancy. And till they be convinced of that error, cannot you have church communion with them?"

ANSWER. To this I answer, I dare not say, but precious souls to God in these times, as well as formerly, may be, in that point, in darkness. I do not censure the case of such. But sure I am that if they judge their own baptism or sprinkling in their infancy to be an ordinance of God, they cannot but judge it a duty still to practice the same upon their own infants, being faithful to their principle. And then how can a church and true ministry that judges dipping of believers a duty, and the other to be a grievous and provoking sin, admit such a person into communion that resolves to live not only in the neglect of a solemn duty, but in a great and heinous sin in the judgement of that church and ministry, that is, to admit him, which the justifying of his baptism must needs be?

Wherefore hath Christ set up in his gospel-church his ordinance of excommunication or casting forth out of the church, if that persons may be admitted that are resolved to live in both a sin of omission and commission, and such as have not repented of that sin of sprinkling children?

So then, that person that lives impenitently in any one known sin—known I mean to the church—, if that church have communion with that person in that sin, the sin becomes the church's sin.

OBJECTION

But he liveth in this sin through ignorance.

ANSWER. That we presuppose, or else the Scripture would send us little hopes of charity as to his good estate. For to know a sin to be a sin, and to live in it, doubtless it cannot stand with grace. Therefore, it is generally concluded that the contempt of any ordinance of God is damnable, but not the simple neglect of it, being upon scruples or doubts of conscience unanswered. But the church knows it to be a sin, and therefore they are not to have communion with it.

OBJECTION

But may some say, "I am afraid some persons do rest in ordinances and place that in them which is due to Christ only, which is some offence to me, and hath kept me off from that practice."

ANSWER. There is no sound ground for this objection from either our profession or practice, for we do profess salvation, justification, and the spiritual welfare to be merely of the grace of God in Christ, and that by faith only, and that our obedience to Christ ought to be performed from a principle of regeneration and union with Christ by faith. And answerable is our practice in that we dare not put any soul on obedience, but from that root. For before we baptize any soul, we prove whether a true work of conversion be wrought in his heart or no, and whether he have union with Christ, and dare not admit children, because that we judge that they have not a principle of Christ in them, from whence they should submit to baptism.

And further, let me say, that it is easy for a soul to forbear resting in duties that doth not perform them. But that which is worthy in a Christian is to walk as strictly in obedience to all the commands of God as though he would be saved by his obedience, and to rest as fully upon Christ and his blood and the love of God therein revealed as if he had done nothing at all, accounting himself an unprofitable servant. And whereas you say you fear they rest in duties, that fear and jealousy in you, I fear, is your sin, and possibly may flow from that inbred enmity and prejudice that is apt to be in every man's heart against the pure ways of God, or else it proceeds from the malice of the devil suggesting such thoughts into thy heart. For thou enter into the hearts of such people and judge their very intents in this, thy fear and jealousy, and therefore beware of this snare.

But further, suppose some souls should be so far left of God that walk in the practice of ordinances as to rest in them—is that a ground for thee to excuse thee, to live in a sinful neglect of them? In a word, there can be no objection come into thy heart tending to hinder thee from this duty and to keep thee from thy obedience to thy Lord and King, but it must needs be from the flesh or from the devil, and therefore beware of them. Suppose thy judgement inclined to such a latitude, as that thou couldst have communion with unbaptized persons. Consider with a tender conscience what hath been said, and I hope it may much satisfy thee in that objection.

But suppose thou shouldst not be satisfied with what hath been said, but still judge that thy liberty. Thou canst not but say it is clear in the New Testament, and out of doubt, that such believing and being baptized ought to have church fellowship together with the practice of ordinances. And is that a justifiable argument to keep thee off from communion with such, as, out of doubt, thou mayest, according to rule have communion with, and further that thou canst not but say is thy duty to have communion with?

Therefore, I would, in all tenderness, admonish and warn all that fear God to be more conformable and observe the rules of Christ, and not to harbour such a gross error in thy mind as to think thou mayst, at thy pleasure, dispute the commands and ordinances of Christ.

The apostle Paul in Galatians 1:16 saith he conferred not with flesh and blood, but he presently obeyed the heavenly voice. And Christ, when God by his Spirit directed him to go to the doctors in the temple to hear them and ask them questions, he without so much as acquainting his father or mother, obeyed the Lord, though to their great grief and trouble in going. And then in Philippians 2:14, our obedience should be without murmuring, repining or any more ado.

And Luke 5:5; Peter had been fishing all night and caught nothing, therefore had little hopes to catch any fish. Yet saith he, "Nevertheless at thy word I will let down the net." He did not dispute the commands of Christ, though his own experience and skill did utterly testify against what Christ had commanded, as to sense, that there could be no good effect produced. Yet at thy word, saith he, I will cast in my net.

As David in Psalm 119:60, "I made haste, and delayed not to

keep thy commandments." For delaying of obedience doth harden the heart and give place to the tempter. And therefore, I would advise all godly souls to drink in this as a maxim: that if you find an express law of Christ given to a believer, it is utterly unlawful to dispute or to question the practice of it upon any pretense whatsoever, or to admit any objection against it.

For amongst men, both in civil and military authority, they will not have their laws disputed, who may err greatly in making those laws. But our righteous God, whose laws be sure are just, will not have his disputed. And therefore, as before, when Christ bid Peter cast down his net into the sea, saith he, "Master, we have toiled all the night, and have taken nothing: nevertheless at thy word I will let down the net." Where observe, though what Christ commanded him, his skill, experience, and reason might have strongly objected against, yet he learned this, that there could not be any justifiable ground to bear him out in disputing Christ's laws.

And thus you have an example in Abraham in sacrificing Isaac, who was the promised seed. "When he was called to go out into a place which he should after receive for an inheritance, obeyed; and he went out, not knowing whither he went."[29] And Noah, when he built an ark for the saving of his house. And Jacob, upon the command of God, carrying away his family three days journey before Laban, and the family knew of it. There might have been much dispute against these things, but these holy men of God had learned not to give place to the pride and rebellion of their unmortified reason and understanding, which many souls,

---

[29] [Heb. 11:8.]

for want of more grace and soundness of judgement, give way to in our days. But they did obey the word of God's command without any more ado, as the apostle's rule is,

> Wherefore, my beloved, as ye have always obeyed, not as in my presence only, but now much more in my absence, work out your own salvation with fear and trembling. For it is God which worketh in you both to will and to do of his good pleasure. Do all things without murmurings and disputings: That ye may be blameless and harmless, the sons of God, without rebuke, in the midst of a crooked and perverse nation, among whom ye shine as lights in the world.[30]

---

[30] Phil. 2:12–15.

FINIS

INDEXES

SCRIPTURE INDEX

174

176

The Particular Classics Series aims to introduce the laity, pastor, and scholar to the classic works of the Particular Baptists. The works included in the series have been carefully selected to both reflect the best of the literature. It is our hope that these selected works will whet the appetite and summon Baptists to take up and read, to discover our Baptist fathers, and recover a heritage that has been buried for far too long.

Printed in Great Britain
by Amazon

85331302R00122